IN GOD WE TRUST

Stories of Faith
in American History

Timothy Crater & Ranelda Hunsicker
Illustrated by **Drew Rose**

ChariotVICTOR
PUBLISHING
A DIVISION OF COOK COMMUNICATIONS

To Nellie Crater, R.N.,
who gave life itself to my late brother,
David Wayne Crater,
and to me,
and who has meant so much to so many
other young people throughout her life.
T.C.

To Marian Bray,
my encourager,
who made this book possible.
R.H.

Chariot Books is an imprint of ChariotVictor Publishing
A division of Cook Communications, Colorado Springs, Colorado 80918
Cook Communications, Paris, Ontario
Kingsway Communications, Eastbourne, England

IN GOD WE TRUST: STORIES OF FAITH IN AMERICAN HISTORY
© 1997 by Cook Communications.

Design/Art Director: Andrea Boven
Illustrator: Drew Rose
Project Editor: Jeannie Harmon

First printing, 1997
Printed in the United States of America
01 00 99 98 97   5 4 3 2 1

CONTENTS

Part One—New Beginnings (1000–1600)

Part Two—The Colonial Period (1607–1765)

Part Three—The Birth of a Nation (1765–1783)

Part Four—Creating a New Government (1783–1817)

Part Five—America Grows Up & Spreads Out (1817–1860)

Christianity and faith in God as the driving force in creating America, shaping its destiny as a beacon of freedom to the world.

Not every single American leader was a person of strong faith. But with very few exceptions, the shining names in American history are the names of people of deep conviction.

If you read today's textbooks, you will learn far too little about religion in American history. You will read that the settlers of New England sought religious freedom. You might learn that religious toleration was the founding principle of Rhode Island, or that Maryland was created as a haven for Roman Catholics. Then, as a rule, religion will vanish from the book's account of the American adventure. What a tragedy! Such textbooks are like a history of the American Revolution that stops with the battle of Lexington.

The authors of this book have done a wonderful thing for America. They present to us the lives of great men and women in the fullness of their faith in God. They show us that America was founded upon faith in God. They remind us that what is great and good in this nation flows from the wellspring of our faith in God.

One of the great historians of antiquity said that his work was "an everlasting possession, not a prize composition that is heard and forgotten." What is great and good never changes, but it can be forgotten. It is my hope that this book will become a key for you to the everlasting possession of love for the United States of America, and a full appreciation that our nation's greatness and security rest upon faith in God.

Hon. John Ashcroft
U. S. Senator—Missouri

INTRODUCTION

Down through our nation's history, men and women have taken a stand for what is right. They came to the New World seeking religious freedom, and found that their faith in God played a role in many life-changing decisions—in discovering new territories, in setting up new governments, in establishing what was fair and just for all.

Over the past century much of this religious heritage has been taken out of our history books, and the influence which faith in God has in the life of an individual has been devalued or ignored. As a result, any discussion of personal faith in our lives and the lives of our forefathers is absent from public school classrooms today. We are in danger of losing our true heritage because the whole story is no longer being told.

In God We Trust presents accurate accounts from the lives of fifty people in the history of our nation. But this is not a boring history book; these accounts are fun and exciting! Each of the narrative stories focuses on how that person's faith in God played an important part in the development of America. These men and women were of differing backgrounds and nationalities, but they brought to our nation a collective heritage of faith in God which stands the test of time and allows us our freedom of religion today.

You'll see how their faith affected their career choices, how they chose to serve others, and the long-term contributions they may made for all of us. Their stories will build your faith and help you to know that God played a big part in the history of America, as He continues to do today.

Also included in this book are facts about where you might find sites to visit that will help you know these people and their history better. A glossary at the back of the book will help define words that you may not know, and the bibliography will provide additional titles if you want to learn more about the people in this book.

We hope you will enjoy reading about faith in action!

Leif Ericson, Missionary Viking

A.D. 1000

Leif stood beside his father on the deck of the longboat. The sleek ship cut a path in the waves as it sailed rapidly toward their home. Greenland. His father had chosen a good name for the new land he had discovered.

The boy with sun-bleached hair and experienced sea legs gazed with pride at his father's Viking helmet. A mane of red hair flowed from under it. Once his father had been forced to flee from Iceland because of a terrible family feud, but now Eric the Red was a very important and respected man.

Someday I will be strong as a mountain, swift as a hawk, and fierce as a bear, Leif thought, *just like Father. Then I will sail the world. Perhaps I too will find a new land.* Leif's daydreams were cut short by the shouts of family and friends as the longboat sailed into its home port. For now the adventuring was over. It was time to return to his farm chores.

"Don't wear such a long face, Leif!" his father said. "We will set sail again one day soon."

A smile flashed across Leif's fair face. He knew it was true. No Viking could leave the seas for long, especially when there were furs, falcons, and warm woolens to be traded in faraway Scandinavia.

The boy leaped over the side of the docked boat and ran to greet his mother, Thjodhild, and his younger brother, Thorvald. Soon Leif was racing toward their stone house. He was eager for some of his mother's delicious butter and freshly made cheese.

Season followed season, and Leif grew to be a man. He did not have his father's blazing red hair or his terrible temper, but he had his courage

and curiosity. He was always ready for an adventure.

Often the Viking sailors would set their ships toward the home of their ancestors in Iceland and Norway. They needed timber, tools, weapons, grain, and other supplies that Greenland could not provide. In exchange for these things, Leif and his fellow settlers offered goods such as hides, seal oil, and ivory walrus tusks.

On one voyage to Norway, Leif met King Olaf. The year was A.D. 1000 and things were changing in the Viking world. King Olaf had once been a fierce raider who attacked and plundered the people of Europe and the British Isles. Then he became a Christian and returned to Norway, intent on winning his countrymen to his new faith.

Of course, when King Olaf met Leif, he eagerly told him about his Christian beliefs. He encouraged the young sailor to turn from the old pagan gods to the one true God. Leif listened and believed. Soon he shared the king's desire to spread the good news about Christ to the whole world.

During the voyage home to Greenland, Leif and his men were blown off course in a violent storm. As they sailed, strange new lands appeared before them.

The adventurers admired the white sandy beaches. They decided to drop anchor and explore the lovely wooded land beyond. One of the men wandered farther than the rest and came upon some wild grapes. "Look what I found!" he shouted to the others. The sailors also discovered wheat growing in this strange new land. As he looked at the bountiful land around him, Leif knew what he would call it.

"This shall be known as Vinland the Good," he proclaimed. Surely a settlement could be established in this beautiful place. And if Leif had his way, it would be a place where people pledged their loyalty to Christ.

Leif and the crew of his ship were eager to tell the settlers in Greenland about their discovery. So they set sail for home. Along the way, they came across a shipwrecked vessel. The crew was still alive, and Leif rescued them, showing that God's love had come to live in his heart. In gratitude, they offered him the entire cargo of their ship.

When Leif's ship arrived in Greenland, the people cheered. They listened to his exciting stories and looked at his treasure. "Leif, the Lucky! Leif, the Lucky!" they cried. And the name stuck.

True to his promise, Leif began to tell his family and friends about the Christian faith. Some, like Leif's mother, believed and became Christians. Others, like Leif's father, scoffed and remained loyal to their pagan gods.

Leif had many adventures, but none more thrilling than his discovery of Christ and the new land he called Vinland. Because the natives of Vinland did not welcome settlers, Leif lived out his life in Greenland. He was its ruler when he died, and his Christian influence on his people is still visible today.

The Scandinavian people kept the story of Leif's amazing discovery alive for centuries. Few believed the incredible tales, but in 1960 archaeologists found the ruins of a Viking settlement in Newfoundland—the northernmost part of North America.

★ ★ ★ ★ ★ ★

In 1964, the United States Congress asked the President to proclaim October 9 as Leif Ericson Day. This annual event honors Leif's heroic voyage and discovery. When you visit the U.S. Capitol building, be sure to look for the painting of Leif in his storm-tossed ship. And remember that he was thinking of telling others about Jesus!

Stephen Langton, Defender of Justice
1155–1228

I will never allow Langton to serve as Archbishop of Canterbury!" King John swore to his advisors.

"But Your Majesty, surely you won't defy the Pope," one of the counselors protested. "His authority is supreme."

"I don't care if Langton is a friend of the Pope. He's not my choice as head of England's church, and I dare anyone to go against my will."

When Stephen Langton heard the King's verdict, he wasn't surprised. He and all of England knew King John was selfish, mean, and bad tempered. Langton was determined not to become like him, so he quietly waited to see what the Pope would do.

Soon Pope Innocent took action. "Until King John accepts Langton as Archbishop, I forbid England's churches to marry, baptize, or bury anyone."

In response, King John stole much of the church's property in England. Then, the Pope expelled King John from the Christian church and from his throne. He encouraged King John's enemies to attack him.

John didn't want to lose his kingdom, so finally he agreed to the Pope's terms. Stephen Langton took charge of England's churches and acted as a counselor to the king. In his new position of authority, he had an opportunity to help others who were suffering injustice.

One day a group of wealthy men who owned large feudal estates came to see Archbishop Langton. "King John sees the prosperity of our towns and manors, and he wants it for himself," their spokesman said. "Is there some way we can stop him from unfairly taxing us and our tenants?"

Wisely, Langton didn't take sides with the barons or the king. "There's only one way to solve England's problem," he told them. "It must become a nation of law and not of men. We need a list of rules that will protect everyone's rights."

The barons agreed. "But we will need your help," they told Langton. For many days the men talked, argued, and wrote down their ideas. At last they reached an agreement on what rights were most important. The first thing on their list was freedom of the church from government control. In addition, they wanted a guarantee of their property rights, fair trials, no taxation without legal approval, and free trade.

"Thanks to you, we have said it well," one of the barons told Archbishop Langton. "Now let us send our charter to the King and see what he will say."

★ ★ ★ ★ ★ ★

Stephen Langton loved God's Word and devoted his life to its study and teaching. We owe the chapter divisions in our Bibles to him. From the Scriptures, Langton learned about life, liberty, and justice, and so can we!

When King John heard the barons' demands, he was outraged. "Who do they think they are?" he shouted. "I'll never put my seal of approval on this piece of nonsense!"

But the barons refused to be silenced. "Let us throw off this tyrant!" and "Down with King John!" they cried. Then they gathered an army and marched on London.

Soon they captured the city. King John was forced to consider their demands. After four days of talks with leading barons and church leaders, he agreed to honor their charter.

Archbishop Langton smiled as he signed his name to the document. He knew a great victory for justice had been won. What he didn't know was that 600 years later, the Great Charter (Magna Carta) would help Americans create a government with just laws at its heart.

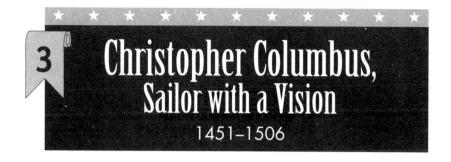

3 Christopher Columbus, Sailor with a Vision
1451–1506

S
o, brother, what secrets do those maps tell you?" Bartholomew asked with a teasing smile. "Have you discovered a secret pathway through the sea?"

Christopher answered with a familiar faraway look in his eyes. "Yes, I am more certain than ever that I can reach Asia by sailing west." His attention quickly returned to the books and charts spread before him.

"Who will ever believe such a wild idea!" Bartholomew said.

"King John, I hope," said Christopher. "I'm almost ready to show him my plan. Surely, he will finance my voyage."

Bartholomew looked doubtful. "Why should he take a chance on your risky proposal?" he said. "Especially when Portuguese ships are successfully reaching Asia by sailing east around Africa."

"Perhaps you are right, brother," said Christopher. "But I will never stop trying. I know my route will work, and one day God will give me success!"

In spite of Christopher's faith, the king of Portugal said no. Then King Henry of England and King Charles of France said no. Determined to win support for his plan, Columbus moved to Spain in search of a royal sponsor.

Soon Columbus made friends with several important Spaniards. One of them helped him get an audience with Queen Isabella. She liked Columbus's idea, but the Spanish experts on sailing didn't. "Ridiculous!" they said, and they laughed at him.

For seven long years, Columbus waited, studied the Bible and other

great books, and prayed. He became more and more certain that God had given him the idea to sail west. "It is as though our Lord has set a fire in my soul," he told his priest. "I feel His hand on me."

In the spring of 1492, his perseverance paid off. Queen Isabella and King Ferdinand agreed to pay for the voyage.

"Oh, thank you!" Columbus said to the rulers and to God. His dream was finally coming true.

Columbus stood on the deck of his ship called the *Santa Maria*. His crew was ready to set sail. So were the men on board the *Pinta* and the *Niña*, two smaller ships in his fleet.

With a broad smile, Columbus shouted, "Weigh anchor!" The date was August 3, 1492, and the adventure had begun.

Three days later, Columbus's faith got a test. The mast of the *Pinta* was damaged badly. The crew of ninety men had to stop for a while in the Canary Islands so they could repair it. On September 6, they set out again, sailing directly west.

One day, Columbus noticed some of his men huddled together. They looked angry, and soon he learned why. "They don't believe I know what I'm doing," he realized. He felt all alone, except he knew God was with him.

As the days passed, the crew's attitude went from bad to worse. Instead of fighting with them, Columbus kept to his course and prayed. "I commit myself to You, Lord. Please complete what You have begun and deliver me safely."

In 1934, President Franklin D. Roosevelt proclaimed October 12 as Columbus Day. When you celebrate Columbus's discovery, remember he preferred to be known as "the Christ bearer," which is the literal meaning of his name.

On October 12, a cry sounded from the crow's nest. "Land ho!" the sailor called. The weary crew rushed to see if it was true. Sure enough, not far away they saw an island, and before the morning ended they set foot on its sandy shore.

"We will call this place *San Salvador* [which means "Holy Savior"] in honor of the Savior who safely brought us here," said Columbus. He and his crew knelt to give thanks while the surprised natives watched.

"O Lord, Almighty and everlasting God," Columbus prayed, "by Your word You created the heaven and the earth, and the sea. Thank You for choosing to use us, Your humble servants, in making Your name known in this second part of the earth."

Columbus was certain God had guided him to Asia. Now we know he had made an even greater discovery than he realized. He had found a New World—America!

Hard times and suffering lay ahead for Columbus. But until his death, he remained convinced, "God made me the messenger of the new heaven and the new earth. . . . He showed me where to find it."

The Valiant Virginians
1607

4

Reverend Robert Hunt groaned as the ship rocked on the stormy waves. He had been seasick for six weeks. Worse still, he and his fellow travelers were still near the coast of England—no closer to America than when they had started their voyage.

"Oh, God, have mercy and speed us on our way," he prayed. "Send us a west wind to fill our sails."

The man caring for Hunt wiped the minister's sweating forehead. "Sir, if you leave the ship and return home, no one will think it wrong," he said. "You have endured enough."

"I have only just begun," said Hunt. "We cannot abandon God's purpose. He will see us through this rough passage."

Day after day, Hunt urged the colonists to look to God for help and strength. "Remember the words we were given when we set sail," he said. "It was written in our instructions, 'The way to prosper and achieve good success is to serve and fear God, the Giver of all goodness, for every plantation which our heavenly Father has not planted will be rooted out.'"

> You can learn more about life in colonial Virginia by visiting the Jamestown Festival Park. There you will see a replica of the original fort and three ships like those that brought Rev. Hunt and his friends to the New World.

Over four months later, as spring of 1607 came to Virginia's coast, Robert Hunt and one hundred other English colonists sighted their new land. The sea-weary travelers were eager to explore, but first they had something more important to do.

Captain Smith told the ship's carpenter and two soldiers to raise a cross on the sandy shore.

Then Reverend Hunt knelt before the cross. Some of the colonists joined him on their knees, and others bowed their heads. "Thank You, God, for bringing us to this land of promise," Hunt said. "Please carry out Your plan through us, we pray in the name of our Savior, Jesus Christ."

When the colonists found what they thought was a good location for their settlement, they began to build a fort and thatched houses. Like planting a seed, they were planting what they hoped would become a successful English community. They called their little village Jamestown in honor of England's King James I (the same King James who gave us the King James Bible).

In the Royal Charter of Virginia, you can discover the colony's purpose: to bring glory to Almighty God and spread the Christian religion to people living in ignorance of the true knowledge and worship of God.

During the next few months, the settlers suffered great hardships. They were attacked by the native Algonquin Indians. Many grew sick and died. Their food supplies ran out, and few of them knew how to farm or hunt. A fire destroyed their newly built fort, several houses, and the church. Then Robert Hunt died.

The fifty remaining colonists gathered to remember this minister they had all loved. "He was an honest, religious, and brave man," one man said.

"He gave up ease at home in order to serve God," a woman added.

One by one, the people raised their voices. "He suffered much, yet never complained." "He comforted us and helped to heal our misunderstandings." "He laid down his life in the foundation of America."

In the days ahead, when the colonists' hearts were most heavy and they did not think they could endure more, God sent help. Ships arrived, loaded with colonists and supplies. The settlers welcomed the newcomers with tears of joy. "God has heard and answered our prayers!" they said.

Over and over through the next few years, the cycle was repeated. Troubles came, prayers brought relief, and thanksgiving rose up to the Lord.

"No matter what happened to Jamestown," Captain John Smith said, "God would not let it be uprooted."

By 1619, the number of colonies in Virginia had increased to eleven. Two representatives were elected in each settlement. These men gathered at the church in Jamestown. The new chaplain, Reverend Richard Buck, greeted them.

"Before the work of this new Virginia Assembly begins," Chaplain Buck said, "let us ask God to guide and bless our work to His glory and the good of this land."

The men reverently bowed their heads. Then they gathered in their church to work on creating Virginia's—and America's—first representative government.

Standing before his fellow Christians, Pastor William Brewster described the proposed journey to the New World. "Are you willing to leave behind your friends? Can you and your children face the dangers of crossing the ocean?"

He waited for them to think about his questions. Then he continued. "Are you ready to learn new ways of making your living? And what if you and your families are attacked by the natives of this strange land?"

After a brief silence, one man said, "We are ready." Then another spoke, "Our trust is in God alone." Speaking for them all, one of the elders added, "We must be free to worship the Lord in purity and truth, no matter what it may cost us!"

And so it was decided to sail to America. The band of Christians purchased a small ship called the *Speedwell*. Since the *Speedwell* wasn't big enough to hold everyone, they paid for several of their group to travel on another larger ship called the *Mayflower*.

When you visit the Capitol Building in Washington, D.C., look for the painting of the Pilgrims kneeling on the deck of the *Speedwell*, a copy of the New Testament of Our Lord and Savior Jesus Christ lying open in the center of the praying pilgrims.

Before they began their journey, they spent a day in prayer and fasting. Then they said good-bye to their friends and boarded the ships.

Not far from the coast of England, the *Speedwell* began to leak. The ship's captain told the people, "I must turn back! The ship will soon sink if we sail on."

The passengers on the *Speedwell* decided to join those on the *Mayflower*, and their voyage to Virginia finally began. In spite of their problems, they gave thanks to God for clear weather and a good wind.

Not everyone on board shared the Christian faith of William Brewster and his congregation. Some of passengers and the ship's crew actually hated them for their beliefs.

One of the sailors cursed the Christians. When he saw them seasick, he would say, "I'll be helping to bury half of you in the sea before too long."

They prayed for him, but he did not change. Strangely, that sailor became sick and was the first to be thrown overboard.

The rest of the sailors were frightened by this. "It is God's hand upon him for cursing these good people on board," they muttered to each other.

As the *Mayflower* continued on its way to Virginia, storms threatened to sink it. Again the pilgrims prayed and the ship survived. But the strong winds had blown it off its course. It wasn't headed toward Virginia anymore as their royal charter required.

★ ★ ★ ★ ★ ★

You can read about the Pilgrims and their many adventures in William Bradford's own words. His book, *Of Plymouth Plantation*, was the first history book written in America.

"Shall every man do as he wishes in this new land?" some of the Pilgrims asked.

Their leaders quickly responded, "No, we must form a new government to guide our colony." So several of the men gathered in the ship's cabin and wrote the Mayflower Compact.

When they returned to the deck, they gathered the people and read the document. It said, "Having undertaken for the glory of God and the advancement of the Christian faith and honor of our king and country, a voyage to plant the first colony in the northern part of Virginia, we do, solemnly and in the presence of God and of one another, agree to form a governing body, for our better ordering and preservation, and the further-ance of our goals."

The men on board signed the new agreement, promising they would live in obedience to the laws of the Mayflower Colony.

On a cold winter day in December, the *Mayflower* landed at Cape Cod, Massachusetts. The weary pilgrims fell to their knees on the shore. "Thank You, God, for bringing us over the ocean!" Some of them cried for joy. "Thank You, Father, for protecting us and bringing us to this good land."

The newcomers decided to settle at a place called Plymouth. That first winter in Massachusetts brought death to more than half of them. But those who lived began to plant gardens in the spring.

Then their governor grew sick and died. They elected William Bradford to take his place. No matter what happened, they didn't intend to leave.

Soon they made friends with some Native Americans who showed them new ways of hunting, fishing, and farming. After their first harvest, the Pilgrims gathered to celebrate America's first Thanksgiving Day.

John Winthrop, Godly Governor
1588–1649

The summer sun was bright as attorney John Winthrop and his friend rode through the English countryside to a Puritan gathering. The men talked about their children and grandchildren. Then their thoughts turned toward the future and what it held for their families.

Suddenly, Winthrop felt his horse lurch under him. Too late, he realized it had lost its footing. The horse fell, throwing Winthrop into a swampy hole. Water came up to his waist, and the mud under his feet sucked him down. With his friend's help, he struggled free.

"Thank the Lord for protecting me!" Winthrop exclaimed.

After he had recovered from his fall, Winthrop turned to his trusted friend and said, "I think England is more dangerous than this swampland. It's sunk in its sins and trying to pull us down too!" His face filled with sorrow. "Downing, I see dark days ahead."

"So do I," Emanuel Downing replied. "King Charles has no use for Puritans. He believes it is his divine right to rid England of us. No doubt it is because of your beliefs that you have lost your position in the court."

When you visit the U. S. Capitol building in Washington, D.C., you can see a statue of John Winthrop in the hallway beneath the chamber of the House of Representatives.

"Yes, and now that Bishop Laud is allied with the King, we are in even more danger," Winthrop said. "Just as King Charles has dismissed Parliament and locked up those who oppose him, Laud will persecute any who reject his regal religious ceremonies and traditions."

"Shall we join those leaving for America next spring?" Downing asked.

Winthrop nodded. "I see that as our only hope. Perhaps God has provided this place as a refuge . . . a place where we can build a *new* England. Let us pray the Almighty will give us a better life there."

Soon, John Winthrop agreed to lead a venture called the Massachusetts Bay Colony. He used his clear thinking and his powerful way with words to encourage other Puritans to join him. Many of the colonists were wealthy and well-educated. Some were artisans and merchants. Others were scholars. All of them had two things in common: they wanted to worship God in the way they believed the Bible taught, and they were eager to tell others about Jesus Christ.

On a wall in the Library of Congress, you will find one of John Winthrop's favorite Bible verses: "What doth the Lord require of thee, but to do justly, and to love mercy, and to walk humbly with thy God" (Micah 6:8). It is a good creed for all Americans.

The following March, six shiploads of Puritans set out for New England. On board the *Arbella*, Winthrop had plenty of time to think and pray. He carefully wrote a description of the New England Puritans' covenant with God. Then he presented his message to those on board.

"Since we are fellow members of Christ, we should live together in love," Winthrop said. "God has guided us to seek out a place where we can live and work under a common government. In this effort, we must put the good of the public ahead of our private interests."

Winthrop's listeners nodded their agreement. He went on to tell them that others would be watching their example to see if their lives improved and they could do more for the Lord. "The eyes of all people are upon us."

When the colonists reached New England, they built a thriving settlement called Boston. These courageous people took a stand for morality, and they based their laws on God's commandments. For nineteen years, John Winthrop served as their governor. Just as he had hoped, thousands of Puritans heard about the Massachusetts Bay Colony and came to New England.

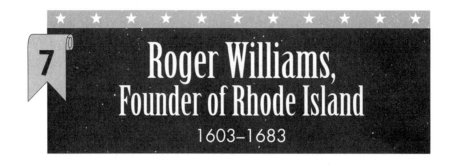

7 Roger Williams, Founder of Rhode Island
1603–1683

I
s this how you repay my kindness?" Sir Edward Coke said. "You could be a brilliant lawyer or a respected minister. But now you're throwing it all away to join a bunch of religious fanatics!"

Roger Williams quietly waited until the storm of words ended. He had known Sir Edward would be furious over his decision to join the Puritans in their fight for church reform. He said, "I am deeply grateful for what you have spent on my education. And I am even more thankful for your friendship. But, Sir Edward, I must obey my conscience."

It was a hard choice for the young man to make because he loved his benefactor. But he was convinced that England's church was corrupt. He wanted to do whatever he could to bring it back to a true worship of God.

Since Roger was a likable young man, he made friends easily. And he shared his ideas with everyone. This soon got him into trouble with powerful men. To escape going to prison, he quickly left England.

During the voyage to America, Williams spent most of his time studying the Bible. He decided being a Puritan reformer wasn't enough. "We will never change the Church of England. We must break away and start a new church with God's Word as our only Guide."

When Roger Williams arrived in Boston, Governor Winthrop and other leaders gave him a warm welcome. "We're in need of a minister right now," they told him. "Will you come and preach for us?"

"I must refuse your kind offer," Williams said politely. "I cannot serve in a church that is still joined to the Church of England."

The Puritans were shocked and insulted. They feared the young man would bring trouble to New England.

Soon Williams received an invitation to teach in the Salem, Massachusetts, church. But the Boston Puritans warned their friends in Salem that the new preacher was dangerous.

Eventually Williams decided that Plymouth Colony and its church would be a better place for him and his family. The Pilgrims there shared more of his beliefs.

In Plymouth, Williams learned to farm and hunt. He also made friends with Native Americans in the area and learned their language. The Wampanoag and Narragansett chiefs liked Williams, and found him to be trustworthy. As he talked and traded with them, Williams thought about how the white people had stolen their land. He decided it was time to speak up for them.

"How can the King of England give you land for your colony when he does not own the land himself?" Williams asked the Pilgrims and Puritans. "No one ever paid the Indians anything or even asked their permission to be here."

This wasn't the only thing about New England that Roger Williams criticized. "The magistrates have no right to punish people for sins against God. They should deal only with wrongs against men and women, or against the community," he said.

In spite of his unpopular ideas, the church in Salem invited Williams to come back and be their pastor. He agreed, and for a while things went well. In addition to his church work, Williams started a successful trading company. Everything would have been fine if he had only stayed quiet about his beliefs. But he didn't.

★ ★ ★ ★ ★ ★

The Charter of Rhode Island, 1663

No person within the said colony . . . shall be any wise molested, punished, disquieted or called in question for any differences in opinion in matters of religion . . . all and every person and persons may . . . enjoy his and their own judgments and consciences in matters of [religion], they behaving themselves peaceably and quietly, and not using this liberty to [commit immorality or irreverence], nor to the civil injury or outward disturbance of other.

The Massachusetts governors, magistrates, and ministers decided it was time to make Roger Williams be quiet. So they ordered him to appear in court.

"Since you persist in spreading many strange and dangerous opinions that oppose our authority, we order you to leave Massachusetts. You have six weeks to secure passage or the magistrates will remove you by force."

Williams returned home to Salem. He was very sick, but he continued to talk to everyone who visited him about the errors in the Massachusetts government.

Outraged, the magistrates sent soldiers and a ship to take Williams back to England. But just before they reached Salem, Williams escaped on foot. For four days he walked with a snowstorm whirling around him. At last he reached the village of his friend Chief Massasoit. "You are welcome with us!" the chief said.

When spring came, Williams, along with some Englishmen who had joined him, began a new settlement. He tried to buy the land from the Narragansett tribe, but they insisted on giving it to him.

"God has shown merciful providence to me in my distress," Williams said. "Therefore, we will call this new settlement Providence. It will be a shelter for anyone who is persecuted for reasons of conscience."

In spite of what he had suffered from fellow Christians, Williams remained strong in his faith. But when it was time to set up the government of Providence Plantation and the new Rhode Island Colony, he made sure it included complete religious freedom. His courage helped to guide the men who later wrote our U.S. Constitution.

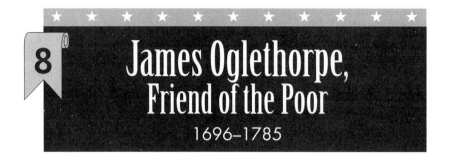

8 James Oglethorpe, Friend of the Poor
1696–1785

Must we sentence the poor to these wretched prisons?" James Oglethorpe said to his friends as they ate dinner. "Surely there is a better way of dealing with those who can't pay their debts."

A portly gentleman sitting beside Oglethorpe spoke up. "What would you suggest? I doubt that the King or we members of Parliament are ready to pay their bills. Anyone who's too lazy to earn a living for himself and his family deserves to rot in prison."

Oglethorpe's unhappy face plainly said that he disagreed. "Many of these prisoners would be glad to pay their debts. But some cannot find jobs, and others are too sick to work." He looked down at his full plate and thought of his friend who had died of sickness and hunger in a debtors prison.

Another of the Parliament members spoke up. "It is sad to see, but we cannot be responsible for the bad luck of everyone in England." Then the men began to talk about fox hunting and other pleasant things.

But Oglethorpe didn't listen. He was still thinking about the terrible conditions in the jails. He didn't like seeing a problem and not doing anything about it.

The next day in Parliament, Oglethorpe stood and spoke to the entire assembly about the debtors prisons. After much discussion, the British lawmakers decided to form a committee to investigate prison conditions.

When the committee saw the prisons and met some of the men inside, they quickly agreed with Oglethorpe that something must be done.

Oglethorpe spoke, "I think I may have a plan." The committee members urged him to continue. "If the King will agree, we could establish a new colony in America—a place where these people could have a new start. Surely risking their lives to help enlarge England's claim on the New World would earn forgiveness of their debts."

Lord Percival, one of the men on the committee, said, "I know someone who would like your idea—Archbishop Thomas Bray. He may be able to help you get the support you'll need."

As soon as he could, Oglethorpe talked to Archbishop Bray about the suffering of debtors in England's prisons. The Archbishop liked Oglethorpe's idea for a debtors' colony. "I will use all my influence to help you gain approval and money for this worthy plan," said Archbishop Bray.

★ ★ ★ ★ ★ ★

Two hundred Lutherans from Salzburg, Austria, fled to Georgia in 1734 to escape persecution. They built a settlement called New Ebenezer on the Savannah River. They also gave Georgia its first church, gristmill, and sawmill. During the Revolutionary War, British troops took the town and used its church as a stable and hospital. After that, New Ebenezer became almost a ghost town. You can learn about the Salzburgers and their life in Oglethorpe's colony by visiting the New Ebenezer museum.

In 1732, James Oglethorpe's request was granted by King George. The land between South Carolina and Florida became the Georgia Colony. Parliament generously supported the new venture.

The following year, Oglethorpe and the first settlers sailed to America. Together they started Savannah, the first Georgia settlement.

In early Georgia, slavery was forbidden. Oglethorpe also made sure that traders couldn't sell rum there. He didn't want a love of liquor among the settlers or the Native Americans to ruin his plans.

Oglethorpe wanted Georgia to be a safe and peaceful place for everyone. He treated the local Creek Indians with respect. He also welcomed persecuted Christians of many different beliefs. Jews found a home in Savannah as well.

One of the most important goals of the colony was spreading Christianity. But Oglethorpe had a hard time getting Anglican priests to come to Georgia. When they came, they often grew sick and died or decided to go back to England.

Then a minister named George Whitefield came to Georgia. His great preaching made people want to know God. They filled the church to hear him. When it became too small for the crowds, Whitefield preached to them in the fields.

In addition to preaching about Jesus Christ, Whitefield built an orphanage near Savanah. He named it Bethesda, which means "house of mercy." It was one more way Georgia became a home for the homeless.

Later at Oglethorpe's urging, John and Charles Wesley (founders of the Methodist church) came to Georgia to begin their ministries in America. John began his ministry in Savannah, Georgia; Charles his ministry in Frederica on St. Simon's Island.

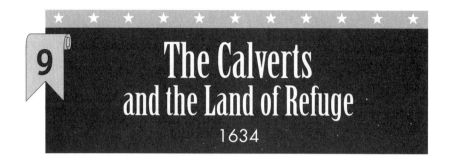

The Calverts
and the Land of Refuge
1634

I am sorry I must leave you, my dear," George Calvert said to his wife. "But I will be back just as soon as King Charles approves my request for land around the Chesapeake Bay."

Fighting back tears, his wife said, "It is clear we Catholics are not welcome here in Virginia. And England doesn't want us either."

"Yes, but King Charles is a true friend," George answered. "I believe he will help us."

George Calvert, also known as Lord Baltimore, had good reasons for believing in the strength of his friendship with the king of England. He had been knighted by Charles' father, King James I, because of his loyal service. When Charles took the throne, he appointed George to a position of great trust in his kingdom.

But a shadow hung over his successful career. He had decided to openly declare his Roman Catholic faith. This took great courage, since at that time it was against the law to practice Catholicism in England. The British wanted only one form of worship in their country—the Church of England (Anglican), with the King of England as its head.

When George admitted he was a Catholic, he lost his job. To help him get a new start, King Charles granted him land in Virginia. The Virginia Company didn't like that at all. So now George hoped to start a settlement north of Virginia.

When he reached England and talked to King Charles, his hopes were rewarded.

"We will call this new province Mary's Land," said the King, "in honor of my wife. Queen Henrietta Maria shares your faith. You and your heirs will be Lord Proprietors."

"This is most generous, Sire," George said. He knew England had never given anyone in America such a powerful position. As Lord Proprietor, he could create a self-governing territory. *I will make it a place of protection for people of all religious faiths*, he thought with joy.

Before the colony charter could be issued, something terrible happened. At the age of only fifty-two, George Calvert died. Cecil Calvert, George's oldest son, inherited the charter.

A young man of twenty-six, Cecil shared his father's dream. But he needed to stay in England to protect the land grant from those who wanted to take it away from the Calverts. So he turned to his twenty-two-year-old brother, Leonard. "Are you willing to go to America and serve as governor of Maryland?" Cecil asked.

★ ★ ★ ★ ★ ★

Thanks to a living history museum, you can learn what life was like for the early colonists in St. Mary's City. There you will find replicas of the State House, a seventeenth century inn, and the ship named the *Dove*. You can also see how archaeologists are digging up more of Maryland's history and visit a recreated Native-American village.

"Of course," said Leonard. He and Cecil immediately began inviting people to join the colony. "I think Father Andrew will go too. And he'll help us talk to others about the colony."

Their priest, Andrew White, wrote to English Catholics, telling them about Maryland. "The English nation, famous for its victories, has never tried anything more noble than this. By sowing the seed of religion in this fruitful land, many thousands of souls will be brought to Christ."

The year after George Calvert's death, Leonard and a group of about 250 settlers sailed for Maryland. When their ships, the *Ark* and the *Dove*, reached Virginia after a long and difficult voyage, the passengers hoped to purchase supplies and visit with the English colonists. But they were turned away, so they quickly sailed up the Potomac River in search of a good spot to settle.

About six miles up the river, they chose a place for the new colony. They named it St. Mary's to honor the mother of Christ and raised a cross in honor of Christ Himself. Then Governor Calvert met with the Native-American tribes in the area. The Yaocomicos, Wicomocos, and Piscataways welcomed the English colonists. They taught them how to fish, hunt, and trade with other tribes. The English shared their tools, seeds, and farming techniques. This friendly exchange helped the colony get a good start.

Many of Maryland's early settlers were called *redemptioners*. This meant they had agreed to work for the Catholic gentlemen who paid their way to America. Some of them were poor working people, others had been sentenced to debtors' prisons, and many had been in jail because of their religious beliefs. They all found a welcome in Maryland.

One of the redemptioners on board the *Ark* was named Mathias de Sousa. After his indenture [time of service] had ended, he became a successful trader. He was selected to serve in Maryland's legislative assembly, and became the first black man to vote in an American legislature.

In 1649, the Calverts' principles of religious tolerance became law. The Act Concerning Religion promised "no person whatsoever within this Province professing to believe in Jesus Christ shall be in any way troubled or persecuted for his or her religion, nor in any way forced to practice another religion."

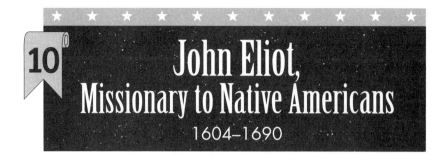

10 John Eliot,
Missionary to Native Americans
1604–1690

It greatly disturbs me that many of our people think the death of the Indians is God's doing," Pastor John Eliot said to his wife Hanna.

"Yes, our neighbor told me yesterday we should be thankful God is clearing the land for His people," said Hanna with a frown.

"It seems they have quickly forgotten one of the main reasons we came to Massachusetts," said Eliot. He reached for a well-worn paper and read from the Colony's first charter. "Whereby our people may be so religiously, peaceably, and civilly governed, as their good life and orderly behavior may win the natives of the country to the knowledge and obedience of the only true God and Savior of mankind."

Eliot laid down the document and shook his head. "It has been fifteen years since those intentions were written. Yet nothing has been done to reach the natives."

"But, dear, how can we tell them about God when we can't understand their language?" his wife asked. "Can you convince more of them to learn English?"

"No, probably not," Eliot said. "But I can certainly learn theirs. I will ask young Cochenoe to help me."

For the next two years, whenever he wasn't taking care of church duties, Pastor Eliot studied the language of the Massachusetts Algonquins. It was very difficult for him, but his desire to tell them about Jesus kept him going.

One fall day in 1646, Pastor Eliot felt ready to talk to the Algonquins. He carefully prepared a sermon, but they didn't find it interesting. Pastor

Eliot kept practicing, and the next time he preached they listened closely. To his delight, many asked about God's Son, the Bible, and the white men's faith. They encouraged him to come and talk to them again soon.

From then on, Pastor Eliot visited a native settlement every two weeks. One day after he told the people of Christ's love, they asked him, "Why has no white man ever told us these things before?"

The question made Pastor Eliot sad. He was more determined than ever to share God's Word with those who would listen. He also invited other pastors and men from his church to go with him.

As the months went by, Governor Winthrop and other leaders heard about Eliot's work and came to see what was happening. Curious Native Americans from other settlements traveled to hear Eliot preach. Sometimes as many as 200 gathered, and many were converted.

★　★　★　★　★　★

The first Bible printed in America was John Eliot's Algonquin translation of the Scriptures. This man's love for Native Americans also inspired England's Parliament to form the Society for the Propagation of Gospel in New England—a missionary work that continued long after Eliot's death.

The Christian Indians stopped having powwows. Instead they had morning and evening prayers in their wigwams. They spent Sunday in prayers and quietness. The rest of the time, they worked hard to provide for their families and to become more like Christ.

Meanwhile, Pastor Eliot continued his ministry to the English colonists, translated the Scriptures into the Algonquins' dialect, and trained Indian converts so they could form their own church.

These Native American Christians had a different way of life than the rest of their people. But they didn't fit into the white culture either. So they asked Pastor Eliot to help them get a place of their own. Soon the praying Indians were able to start their town. Within twenty years, they had over 1,100 acres and fourteen *praying towns* in Massachusetts.

To the end of his long life, John Eliot did his best to help Native Americans know about Christ.

11 Father Jacques Marquette, Missionary Explorer
1637–1675

Bonjour, Father Marquette, it's good to see you again," said the fur trader Louis Jolliet. He shook the snow from his feet and entered the little mission. "So you want to go with me in search of the Great River?"

"When spring comes, I will be ready," Father Marquette said. "Until then, we will study our maps, compare the stories we have been told by the Indians, and pray for God's blessing. We both have been exploring this land long enough to know the dangers. If we are to succeed in finding and claiming the Mississippi River for France, we will need His help."

"That is why you are going along as our chaplain," said Jolliet. "We're counting on your prayers. And since you know several Indian languages, you can talk to the tribes we meet, as well as to God."

The Michigan winter seemed long to the eager explorers. At last May came and they began their journey. Five other Frenchmen went along as they paddled across Lake Michigan, and then traveled the Fox River to a Mascouten village.

The Native Americans stared at the white men, surprised to see them making this dangerous trip on the river. Father Marquette drew a map on the ground, and told them, "We are looking for the great river called 'the Father of Waters.' Do you know of it?"

"Yes," the chief answered. "Continue on the Fox River to its end. Then carry your canoes to the west. You will find the Miskous [the Wisconsin River] that flows from the northwest. This is the one you must follow." He looked at them doubtfully. "We will send two of our people to guide you."

On June 15, 1673, Marquette and Jolliet reached the Mississippi River. If flowed slowly and gently south, taking their canoes where white men had never been before.

At night, the explorers went on shore to cook their dinner. They didn't see any people along the river, but they were still afraid of being attacked in their sleep. So, after eating, they returned to their canoes.

"I'm beginning to wonder if I will find anyone to tell about Christ," Father Marquette complained. "In such a wonderful place for fishing and hunting, surely there must be some tribes."

Then one evening, they noticed footprints.

"Let's go see where they lead," Jolliet said. Father Marquette eagerly agreed.

The two explorers told the others to wait for them. Following a narrow path, they saw a village ahead of them on the bank of a river. They spotted two others villages on a hill not far away.

Jolliet whistled through his teeth. "Must be 300 cabins out there. There could be thousands of Indians living in them."

"Let us stop and ask God to help us and protect us before we go farther," Father Marquette said. They quietly prayed and then walked silently toward the settlement. When they were close enough to hear voices, they stopped and shouted to let the Indians know they were there.

The people rushed to see the strangers. Four of their leaders stepped forward to greet Marquette and Jolliet. They held out beautifully decorated tobacco pipes without saying anything. Then the Peoria tribe prepared a feast of buffalo meat, corn, and fish.

Further down the Mississippi River, the explorers received a very different greeting. Near the Arkansas River, fierce warriors waved their hatchets, clubs, and bows at them. Some of them ran to their canoes and pushed out into the river.

"They're going to attack us!" Jolliet yelled. Marquette waved the peace pipe given to them by the Peorias, but it didn't seem to help.

Then suddenly, the tribal elders ordered the young men to stop. They motioned with their hands for the Frenchmen to come to shore. Marquette tried all six of the Indian languages he knew, but they didn't understand. Finally, they found an old man who spoke the language of the Illinois tribe (a language Marquette knew). He acted as their interpreter.

After several days in the Arkansas village of Quapaw, the Frenchmen decided to leave. "If what these natives have told us is true," Marquette said, "we are very near the gulf of Mexico. I think we can be sure at this point that the Mississippi flows south unto it."

"If we go much farther, we may find ourselves on Spanish land," Jolliet said. "I think we should turn back now."

On their journey home, the Frenchmen explored the Illinois River. They saw huge prairies and forests, deer, buffalo, turkey, grain, and fruit trees. They also met the friendly Kaskaskia tribe.

In October, the long trip ended. Marquette and Jolliet had traveled 4,000 miles and suffered many hardships.

When spring came again and Father Marquette had recovered from an illness, he decided to travel back to the Kaskaskia village. He took some helpers with him to start a mission. After a short time there, he became ill. He said good-bye to the Kakaskias and headed back to his old mission above Lake Michigan. He died on the way, one of many brave priests who risked their lives to spread Christianity in the New World.

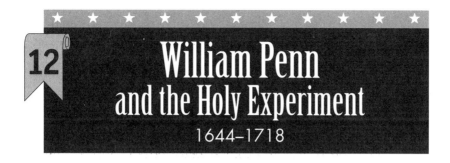

William Penn
and the Holy Experiment
1644–1718

Williliam Penn felt happiest with a quill in his hand. It never took him long to fill a blank sheet of paper with his ideas and beliefs. His pen flew across the page as he wrote to a friend about his new dream.

"I would like to conduct a holy experiment in America," Penn wrote. "If I had a colony of my own, I would make it a place of true Christian and civil liberty. No one would be put in prison for their beliefs."

A colony of his own seemed like an impossible dream, but Penn continued to think about the possibility. Although his Quaker faith called for a simple way of life, it didn't keep him from using his skill in business and politics. He watched for an opportunity to make his dream come true.

England's King Charles owed the Penn family a large sum of money. So William suggested that the King pay his debt by giving William land in America.

King Charles gladly said yes. "You may have the land between New York and Maryland," he told Penn.

"I would like to call the place Sylvania," Penn said, "because it is a lovely wooded land."

"Then it shall be *Pennsylvania* [meaning "Penn's woods"], in honor of your brave father Admiral Penn," said King Charles.

William was a humble man, and he worried that people would think he had named the colony after himself. But the King refused to change it.

Overjoyed with his new opportunity, Penn began telling everyone he knew about Pennsylvania. "I looked to the Lord for it, and I owe it to His hand and power," he wrote to a friend. "I believe He will bless and make it the seed of a nation. I will be careful to set up a good government there."

Penn advertised his new colony throughout Europe. He promised settlers religious freedom, cheap land, and a voice in their own government.

Then Penn wrote a constitution for his colony. In *The Frame of Government*, he said, "government seems to me a part of religion itself, a thing sacred in its institution and end. Although it does not remove the cause of evil, it can crush the effects of evil. In a small way, it shows the power of God."

★ ★ ★ ★ ★ ★

In Pennsylvania, you can find many signs of its founders' Christian faith. For example, Pennsylvania is called "The Quaker State" because of the religious beliefs of its founder. The city of Philadelphia is named for an ancient city in the Bible. William Penn chose this name because it means "brotherly love."

To further guard the religious freedom of Pennsylvania, Penn created a Charter of Liberties. "No people can be truly happy if they cannot follow their consciences," he wrote. "So I guarantee that no one living in this province . . . will be persecuted in any way for their beliefs."

William Penn was a Christian in his actions as well as his words. He insisted on buying the land from the Native Americans. He wrote them a letter promising to treat them with respect and fairness. He insisted that all the Pennsylvania settlers follow his example. When he came to America, Penn quickly made friends with the Indians and negotiated a peace treaty—one he never broke.

Many groups of people found a true friend in William Penn. Quakers, Catholics, Mennonites, Lutherans—they were all welcome in Pennsylvania.

Unfortunately, not everyone in Penn's province shared his integrity and goodwill toward others. Many of them fought. Some government leaders were dishonest and greedy. In the wilderness, people often settled their arguments with guns. In addition, settlers borrowed money from Penn and never repaid him. And there were boundary disputes with neighboring colonies.

This was a great disappointment to William Penn. He thought his holy experiment had failed. But it hadn't. Penn's commitment to peace and religious freedom paved the way for a *United* States of America.

13 Eusebio Francisco Kino, Western Explorer
1645–1711

"Where would you like to take the good news about our Savior, Father Kino?" asked one of the young Italian's fellow priests.

"Perhaps to China," said Kino thoughtfully. "Our Jesuit missionaries are finding some success there by combining preaching with instruction in science and mathematics."

"Then certainly that is the place for a gifted math teacher like you," his friend said with a smile.

"The place for me," Kino corrected, "is wherever God and His church send me."

After many years of study and preparation, the time came for Kino to receive his missionary assignment.

"Oh, God, please direct me according to Your will," he prayed. Then he and other priests reached into a basket and drew out slips of paper. Kino read his slip. "New Spain." Someone else would be going to China, and he would sail to Spanish America.

In 1681, Kino arrived in the strange new world where he had been assigned. The priests in charge of Spanish American missions met with him and explained the work he would be doing. "Father Kino, we understand you are quite an expert in mathematics

You can learn more about Father Kino and his missionary work among the Pima tribe by visiting San Xavier Indian Reservation near Tucson, Arizona, and Tumacacori National Historical Park near Arizona's border with Mexico.

and astronomy," one of the elder priests said. Kino nodded and tried not to look proud.

"As you may know, there are few maps of this land," his superior continued. "We are counting on you to draw maps for us so we can decide where to build churches and settlements. Of course, to do this, you must travel through unknown and dangerous country. But since it is for the cause of Christ, I'm sure you will welcome the job."

Kino made his first missionary journey the next year. He traveled on horseback from Mexico City to Baja, California. The Spanish believed Baja was an island and they wanted to start a mission settlement there.

On the way to Baja, Kino saw many amazing new sights. "Look at those strange plants!" he said to the priests who traveled with him. "They look like the pipes of great organs in Europe's cathedrals!"

★ ★ ★ ★ ★ ★

You can find a statue of Eusebio Kino in the U.S. Capitol building, in the hallway under the U.S. House chamber. The state of Arizona placed it there to honor this great missionary explorer.

During his exploration, Kino discovered Baja, California was a long, narrow peninsula connected to the American continent. He made careful maps of the area and began telling the native tribes about the Christian faith. Before his work got very far, he received a message that Spain wanted to give up the mission.

"Well, it seems God wants me in Pimería Alta [southern Arizona and northern Sonora]," Kino told his fellow priests one day in 1687. He prepared for the trip and headed for a river valley farther north than any other Spanish missionary had gone.

With the help of Indian guides, Kino and his assistants found a good place for the mission. They named it Nuestra Señora de los Dolores. "This is a fine place for raising cattle," Kino said. "And we can also teach the Pima tribe to plant orchards and vineyards."

These projects went well, but Kino couldn't stay in one place very long. In spite of the dangers, he enjoyed exploring. He followed the river valleys farther north and west, making sketches that later became maps.

On one of his trips, he discovered the ruins of four-story Indian *pueblos* [villages] that had been deserted for over 200 years.

Wherever Father Kino went, he told Native Americans about Jesus Christ. He wasn't like some of the Spanish explorers and priests who only wanted their treasures and slave labor. Kino was a true friend to the Pimas and other tribes. Thousands of them listened to his teaching and were baptized into the Christian faith.

For twenty-five years, Eusebio Kino traveled and planted missions. During his lifetime, he made over forty trips and traveled about 50,000 square miles, exploring the Southwestern deserts, mountains, and rivers. His maps helped the Spanish build roads and increase their settlements in North America.

14 Father Junípero Serra, Missionary to California
1713–1784

You look very sad today, Father Serra," said Francisco Palóu. "Is something wrong?"

"I believe God wants me to become a missionary to New Spain," said Serra to his former student, who was now his best friend.

"But you are one of our finest teachers!" said Palóu. "Your knowledge and training would be wasted in such a primitive land."

Serra shook his head. "When I heard Father Mezquía talk about the need for missionaries to the Pame Indians, I began to wonder if God wanted me to go," Serra said. "It is very hard to think of leaving beautiful Majorca and my family and friends. My parents are old and I would never see them again." His eyes filled with tears. "But I remember Christ's words. Our Savior said, 'Anyone who prefers father or mother to me is not worthy of me.'"

"Perhaps there will be enough volunteers without you," said Palóu. He wanted to reassure his friend, whom he admired greatly. But secretly, he also wondered if he should become a missionary too.

In early 1749, both men received a message from Father Mezquía. "Five of the priests who agreed to go to the New World have backed out. Would you like to take two of their places?"

Serra and Palóu said yes. Before he sailed from Spain, Serra wrote a friend with a message for his parents. "Tell them it was for the love of God I left them and with His help I found the courage to do it. I hope their love of God will help them be content with my decision."

When Serra and Palóu reached Mexico, they were sent to teach the

Pame tribe of Sierra Gorda about Christianity. For nine years, they served the five missions in the area. Then they received a call to go to Texas, but trouble among the Apache and Comanche tribes changed their plans. Instead, the two priests returned to Mexico City and served in the Roman Catholic school called San Fernando College.

Serra enjoyed training the young priests, directing the choir, and preaching. But he still longed to be a missionary. His prayers were answered when he received a call to supervise the missions in Baja California. He eagerly left Mexico City for the place Spanish soldiers called "the last corner of the earth."

Not long after Serra went to Baja California, he learned of plans for an expedition into Alta California (what is now the state of California). José Galvez, an important Spanish official, told Serra about the plan to settle the area.

"Spain is worried that unless we act soon, Russia may try to claim more land," Galvez explained. "We're hoping that missionaries can help us settle the area and win the Indians' loyalty."

Serra's face glowed with excitement. "My dream is to build missions along the coast of California," he told Galvez. "I would like to join your expedition."

When the time came to leave, Serra was too sick to go along. He had sores on his leg that would not heal. But he didn't give up on his dream. Against the advice of his friends, he began a six-week mule ride through the desert. When he caught up with the expedition, its leader said, "Father Serra, I must insist that you stay behind."

"Your honor, do not speak of that," said Serra. "God will give me the strength to reach San Diego, as he has given me strength to come this far.

Even if I should die on the way, I will not turn back."

Serra had to be carried to San Diego on a stretcher, but he made it there alive on July 1, 1769. The priest exclaimed, "How beautiful!" when he saw the harbor and the green and blossoming land around it. "This is nothing like Baja California. In fact, it reminds me of my homeland."

Later that month Father Serra dedicated the mission. A year later he converted his first Pala Indian to the Christian faith.

In 1770, when Serra heard that an expedition was leaving in search of Monterey,

he joined it. In spite of his advancing age and poor health, he still dreamed of starting missions along the California coast. And his dream came true.

That same year, he founded San Carlos Borromeo (first in Monterey and then it was moved to Carmel). As the years went by, Father Serra kept building his ladder of missions, one step at a time—Mission San Gabriel (Pasadena), Mission San Antonio de Padua (King City), Mission San Luis Obispo de Tolosa (San Luis Obispo), Mission San Francisco de Asis (San Francisco), Mission de Nuestra Señora la Reina de Los Angeles (Los Angeles), and Mission San Buenaventura (Ventura).

Father Serra made his home at Mission San Carlos Borromeo, but he spent much of his time traveling between missions. During the American Revolution, he asked the priests and workers in the missions to pray for the cause of liberty.

At last Serra became too sick to go on. His friend Palóu stayed by his bedside until the end.

"Palóu, if God lets me go to heaven, I promise to pray for all those who continue the work in the missions," Serra said weakly. "And I will pray for a change of heart in those who do not yet share our faith in Christ."

After Serra's death, Palóa and other priests continued adding to the chain of California missions and baptizing its natives into the Christian faith.

15 Eleazar Wheelock
and Dartmouth College
1711–1779

Reverend Wheelock?" the handsome Mohegan said when Eleazar Wheelock opened the door.

"Yes, can I help you, young man?" Wheelock asked.

"My name is Samson Occom," the teenager said. "I'm from the New London area (Connecticut). I've come here to Lebanon because I've heard you teach Indians. I wonder if you would accept me as a student."

Wheelock shook hands with his visitor. "Come in Samson, and tell me more about yourself," he invited.

With a solemn and intense look on his broad face, Samson said, "About two years ago, I heard that God had visited our land in a special way. I wanted to know more, so I listened to the preachers who came and told us how Jesus Christ died for us. I decided this was the true way to God. Now I want to learn how to tell others about Him."

Samson reached into his pocket and took out a folded paper. "Here is a letter from the minister of the New London church. It will help you know that I speak the truth." He handed it to Wheelock.

The minister read the letter and asked Samson many questions. Finally, he said. "I see you are a very intelligent and sincere young man. You can live here in my home, and I will do my best to help you prepare for missionary work."

For the next four years, Samson studied hard and continued in his commitment to Christ. When the time came for him to leave the Wheelocks, Samson Occom had a thorough knowledge of the Bible, Christian beliefs, the

English language, and public speaking.

"You are ready to go to your people with the good news about Jesus," Wheelock told Samson one day in 1747. "God bless you in your work and send me many more young men like you."

For the next fifteen years, Samson told the Montauk tribe of Long Island about Jesus. In 1759, he became a Presbyterian minister.

Meanwhile, Rev. Wheelock's success with Samson and his concern for Native Americans had inspired him to do more than tutor. "I believe God would be pleased for us to start a school," he told Joshua Moor, a wealthy man in the community. "I would like to train Indians and whites for missionary service. The Indians can learn our ways, and the white men can learn the Indian languages and cultures. But I need someone who is willing to provide money for the school. Would you help me?"

★ ★ ★ ★ ★ ★

Dartmouth College is one of American's most respected schools. When you think of its founder, Reverend Eleazar Wheelock, remember that the Great Awakening of the 1730s and 1740s—a time of tremendous revival in the colonies—caused Americans to become more concerned about education and spreading their Christian faith. For this reason, they started many of America's great schools, colleges, and universities.

Mr. Moor said yes. In addition to money, he donated land and buildings where the school could meet. In 1754, Wheelock began Moor's Indian Charity School with two students. Word spread through New England about this missionary training school, and other students came. Within a few years, twenty-two students enrolled.

As the Indian School grew, so did Rev. Wheelock's dream. He wanted to leave the church he pastored and give all his time to teaching. "I think it would also be good to move the school and try to reach tribes in New York and southern Canada," he told the famous British evangelist George Whitefield.

"Now that the tribes aren't caught up in the war between England and France, it will be easier to share God's Word with them."

"I am most impressed with your ministry to the Indians," Whitefield said. "And I know someone who might be willing to help you. Write to my friend, the Earl of Dartmouth, and ask him to support your school."

Wheelock sat down at his desk later that day and began to write. "March 1, 1764. Your Lordship, you have been mentioned often to me by those in this wilderness who love Christ. The Rev. Mr. Whitefield has encouraged me to write and ask for your help in saving the native people of this land."

The Earl of Dartmouth sent back a generous reply. "Praise God!" Rev. Wheelock said when he read the letter to his family. "The Earl is giving us 10,000 pounds [an amount equal to $12,500 in that day]. Now all we need is a charter from King George."

An old friend of Rev. Wheelock's also helped start the new school. Samson Occom went to England for three years and had great success in telling people about Wheelock's ministry. During that time, he preached hundreds of sermons. When he came back to Connecticut, he brought Wheelock a gift. "Here is 10,000 pounds for your school," he said with a glowing face. Then Samson went back to New York as a missionary to the Oneida tribe.

In 1769 the royal charter arrived, and Eleazar Wheelock opened Dartmouth College in Hanover, New Hampshire. It welcomed Delawares, Iroquois, Mohicans, Montauks, and white men who wanted to become missionaries. Unfortunately, the whites didn't really want to learn about Native American cultures. So gradually, the student body became more and more white. But many Indians did receive an education and became preachers and teachers in their villages.

In a time of much misunderstanding and lack of trust between Native Americans and white settlers, Eleazar Wheelock's effort to bring them together took great courage and love.

16 Jonathan Edwards, New England's Christian Thinker
1703–1758

Jonathan listened carefully as his father preached. He knew he would be expected to remember the sermon and answer questions about it later that day. *And perhaps I'll think of a hard question to ask Father*, Jonathan thought. He enjoyed their talks about the Bible. Sometimes his mother joined them.

"Jonathan, it looks like you will follow in the footsteps of your father, your Grandfather Stoddard, and other fine ministers in our family," she told him one day. "But that means you will have to study hard and go to college."

"You don't have to worry about our boy doing well in his studies," his father said. He chuckled. "He always seems to have his head in a book. And he is quickly learning Latin, Greek, and Hebrew." He looked at his son with love and pride. "Soon his homeschooling will come to an end, and we will have to send him off to college."

When Jonathan had his thirteenth birthday, he enrolled at the Collegiate School of Connecticut [now Yale]. Four years later, he graduated as the top student in his class. Since he was so young, he stayed for two more years of study.

On January 12, 1723, Jonathan made the biggest decision of his life. After much serious thinking, he quietly prayed, "Lord God, I give myself to you. The rest of my life and all that I will ever have is Yours."

"Grandfather, I can hardly believe how the young people of Northampton behave," Jonathan said to Samuel Stoddard. "Since I came to

serve as your assistant pastor, I have seen very little interest among them in true Christianity. They spend their time in parties and drinking, staying out all night, and worrying their parents. Isn't there something we can do?"

Reverend Stoddard shook his head. "For sixty years I have pastored this church," he said. "And I have preached God's Word to these young people, their parents, and their grandparents. I have reminded them why our people came to this land, how they dreamed of building Christian communities. But it is as if they are all sleeping or sick. They do not act on what they hear."

"Then we must find a way to wake them, Grandfather," Jonathan said.

"You are young and impatient, son," Rev. Stoddard said. "In time you will learn, there are some things only God can do. All we can do is plant the seeds of faith. He must send the harvest."

Two years after Jonathan Edwards became assistant pastor of the Northampton, Massachusetts Congregational Church, his grandfather died. The leaders of the church decided to make Jonathan their pastor.

For five years, Jonathan and his wife, Sarah, served the Northampton church without seeing much change. The young minister spent much of his time writing carefully thought-out sermons. He always challenged his listeners to put Christian teaching into practice, but he spoke in a flat, quiet way that didn't excite people.

Then in 1734, his grandfather's words began to come true. After one of Jonathan's sermons, a young woman who was known throughout the town for her bad behavior began to cry and ask God to forgive her. Soon others followed her example.

About six months later, Jonathan said, "Sarah, do you realize, more than 300 have come to Christ in the past six months?"

"Yes, Jonathan, this is what we have prayed for," Sarah said. "I feel as though our whole town is full of God's presence. In almost every home, parents and children are excited about studying the Bible. And they're so eager to tell others how Jesus Christ has changed their lives." Her eyes were bright with joy.

Over the next three years, hundreds of people experienced what Rev. Edwards called "the new birth" and joined the Northampton church. Word spread throughout New England about the revival.

Some ministers thought it was good, and others thought it was bad. But regardless of what they thought, people's lives were changing for the better. Within two years, about 150 churches experienced similar awakenings. It has been estimated that as many as 50,000 people (a sixth of New England's entire population) joined these churches. What happened during the Great Awakening helped the colonies feel as though they were as part of a large plan designed by God for America.

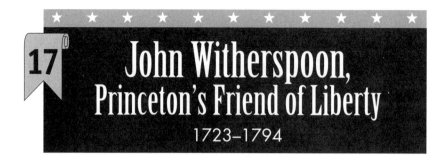

17 John Witherspoon, Princeton's Friend of Liberty
1723–1794

I don't want to go to America!" Mrs. Witherspoon said. She glared at Richard Stockton, the man sent to invite her husband to become president of the College of New Jersey (now Princeton University).

"Why should we risk our lives crossing the Atlantic Ocean?" she continued. "John is pastor of one of the largest churches in Scotland. And the people of Paisley are well educated, not ignorant colonial bumpkins." Her face wore a frown and her voice grew sharp. "Besides, there are dozens of churches and schools much nearer who are begging John to work for them."

Reverend Witherspoon gave Mr. Stockton an embarrassed look. "Please excuse my wife. She isn't feeling well. And as you can see, she isn't eager to leave our home," he said. "Perhaps she will see things differently in time, but for now, I must say no to your kind invitation."

In a few months, another American came to visit the Witherspoons— Dr. Benjamin Rush, who was studying medicine in Scotland. He patiently answered all of Mrs. Witherspoon's questions.

"Well, my dear," Rev. Witherspoon said, "what do you say now about going to America?"

"Perhaps it wouldn't be too bad," she said with a smile. "If that's what you want."

In August of 1768, the Witherspoons arrived in Princeton, New Jersey. "See what a fine land this is," the minister said to his wife. "It is pleasant to the eye and a wonderful place for farming." He looked with admiration at

Nassau Hall, the large building where the college students lived and attended classes.

"I think America is a land of opportunity," Rev. Witherspoon said. "And by training young men in this college, I can make a difference in the future of the colonies."

Under Rev. Witherspoon's leadership, the College of New Jersey rapidly improved and became more popular. He added many interesting new classes, giving students a broader education in languages, logic, history, and public speaking. Soon families throughout the colonies were sending their sons to his school.

During the Witherspoons first few years in America, they heard more and more talk against England. "What do you think about the Stamp Act, Dr. Witherspoon?" people would ask the respected college president. "Is it right for us to be taxed and ordered about by a king and parliament thousands of miles away?"

Witherspoon wouldn't answer. "I don't believe ministers should get involved in politics," he said. But as he watched the unfair way the colonies were treated, he changed his mind. "I will not preach about American liberty," he told his patriot friends, "because I don't think these arguments belong in God's house. But I will put my pen to work for the cause of freedom."

Before long, the man who had been Scotland's most respected minister was called a traitor by the people back home. Rev. Witherspoon didn't let that bother him. Instead, he went on preaching every Sunday in Princeton and directing the business of the college. He also got involved in the Committees of Correspondence, exchanging letters with others who supported American liberty.

Then, in 1776, Witherspoon received a very important invitation from the leaders of New Jersey. "We want you to be one of our delegates at the

Continental Congress in Philadelphia," they told him.

"I will be glad to go," he answered, and he hurried to take his place in the Congress.

When Rev. Witherspoon arrived, the delegates were debating American independence. Some thought the colonies should be loyal to England. Others thought it was time to break away and start their own government.

In the middle of the argument, Witherspoon stood and said, "Some of you have said America is ripe [ready] for independence. But I think the country is more than ripe, and it will soon spoil if we do not take a stand for our freedom."

When the debate ended, the Continental Congress signed the Declaration of Independence. A new nation was born and soon war with England began.

Before the year ended, the British army marched toward Princeton, New Jersey. Just after Thanksgiving, Dr. Witherspoon called the students together and said, "You must all leave now. We cannot have classes in the middle of a battle." Some of the students went home, but many joined the American army.

A week later, the Redcoats invaded Princeton. The Witherspoons had to run for their lives. They took only what they could carry in a little buggy. The British turned Nassau Hall into an army barracks and hospital.

> ★ ★ ★ ★ ★ ★
> "The best friend of American liberty is active in promoting true religion and firm in resisting profanity and evil of every kind. Whoever is an enemy of God is also an enemy of his country."
> —John Witherspoon, 1776

It was a sad time for the Witherspoons, but about a month later General Washington and his troops defeated the British at Princeton. It belonged to the Americans again, and in 1783, while the Continental Congress was meeting in Nassau Hall, England and the United States signed a peace treaty.

The American Revolution caused the College of New Jersey to suffer great losses—to its property, its funds, and its class size. It also cost the

Witherspoons two of their own sons and many students they had grown to love—young men who died fighting for freedom.

After the war, Rev. Witherspoon worked hard to make it a strong school again. He also helped in many ways to shape the United States. In his twenty-six years as college president, 478 students graduated. These young men went on to become leaders in America's churches and government. One became a president, one became a vice-president, and ten served as assistants to the president. Thirteen served as state governors, three were U.S. Supreme Court judges, twenty-one were U.S. Senators, and thirty-nine were U.S. Congressmen.

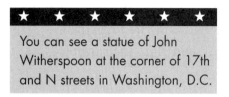

You can see a statue of John Witherspoon at the corner of 17th and N streets in Washington, D.C.

When John Witherspoon died, another great American, John Adams, said, "He was a true son of liberty. But first, he was a son of the Cross."

18 Samuel Adams,
Father of the Revolution
1722–1803

Elizabeth Adams heard the grandfather clock downstairs announce two A.M. Samuel still hadn't come to bed. "That man!" she exclaimed. "Out speaking at one political rally after another, and then writing at all hours of the night!"

A line of soft light shone from under the door of Samuel's study. His wife got up and went to make sure he was dressed warmly enough. As she opened the door, she heard the steady scratching of a quill pen on paper.

"Sam, you need to rest," Elizabeth said. "You're not a young man like those rowdy Sons of Liberty you spend your time with."

He snorted and then replied, "I may be past fifty, but I've still got fire in my bones. And I'm old enough to understand just how much in danger our liberties really are. If we aren't vigilant, England will take away our freedoms one by one until we are little more than slaves."

He stopped speaking as several carriages clattered down the cobbled Boston street. "There go some more of those British revelers!" Sam said in disgust. "They rush from one party or tavern to another in their gilded carriages. Their idle and immoral lives are a bad influence in this city." He shook his head as he thought of the Puritan way of life that had made Massachusetts strong. It flickered now like a candle in the wind.

But Sam would not let that flame go out. He was determined to see Massachusetts, and perhaps all of the colonies, free of English control. He had discovered what mighty weapons his voice and his writing were, and he never let Boston forget the need to fight for their freedom.

When England issued the Stamp Act, he stirred up so much protest, it was repealed. Americans relaxed for a while, until the name of the Townshend Acts brought more taxes and restrictions. British customs officers came to oversee Boston trade. Then two regiments of British soldiers arrived.

Sam angrily remembered the five Americans shot down by the Redcoats. Now the soldiers were gone and so were the intolerable Townshend Acts. He knew it would be easy for Americans to forget the need for vigilance. But Sam would not let them forget. He organized rallies, gave speeches, encouraged the Sons of Liberty in their daring raids, and called on the people of Massachusetts to fast and pray for their land.

Now he had a great new idea for keeping more people informed about English tyranny—the Committees of Correspondence.

He had already formed a Committee in Boston, and others were being organized throughout the colonies. Sam was excited about the idea of Americans pulling together to protect their rights. That excitement kept him at his desk night after night, writing to patriots in Virginia, Pennsylvania, New York, and other colonies.

They needed a document that clearly stated those rights. So Sam was hard at work on The Rights of the Colonists. He reread what he had written so far. "The right to freedom is a gift of the Almighty. . . . The rights of the colonists as Christians are best understood by reading and carefully studying the God-given rights clearly taught in the New Testament."

Sam picked up his pen and continued until he could no longer fight off sleep.

A bronze statue of Samuel Adams stands in front of Boston's Faneuil Hall, where he spoke out for liberty in every town meeting. You can also visit the Old South Meeting House, a Puritan church attended by Samuel and his family. This church was the site of many patriotic gatherings, including the one that started the Boston Tea Party.

Samuel Adams' efforts paid off. Americans became so concerned about British taxation and other restrictions, they decided to hold a Continental

Congress. In September 1774, each colony sent representatives to Philadelphia. Of course, Samuel Adams was there to represent Massachusetts. At last, the colonies were thinking about more than their own problems and best interests. They were beginning to act like a union of states.

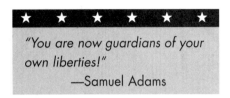

"You are now guardians of your own liberties!"
—Samuel Adams

The next year, Sam was elected to Second Continental Congress. On his way to Philadelphia, the British almost captured him and his friend John Hancock. When the Congress began, Sam stood and said, "It is time to do more than talk. It is time to fight for our independence!"

Not everyone agreed with the fiery Samuel Adams, at least not right away. But he never gave up. With the help of more moderate men like his cousin John Adams, he helped to bring about the United States Declaration of Independence. When it was signed in 1776, Sam Adams said, "We have this day restored the King to whom all men ought to be obedient. He reigns in heaven and from the rising to the setting of the sun, let His kingdom come."

Paul Revere,
Messenger of Liberty
1735–1818

Paul watched closely as his father etched a design of swirling leaves around the edge of a shiny gold button. "It is beautiful, Father!" he said.

Apollos Revere smiled at his son. "You may share your mother's plain Puritan faith, but you have my French blood in you," he said. "It shows in your love of fine things and your curiosity."

His eyes shining with pride, Paul begged, "Tell me again, Father, about how you escaped from France when the King persecuted the *Hugenots* [Protestants]."

"You know the story as well as I, son," Apollos said. "But I will tell it again, and we will both think of what a wonderful place America is."

When Paul Revere wasn't listening to his father's stories and learning his craft, or attending Boston's North Writing School, he played with his friends at the waterfront. All year round, the ships sailed in and out. Paul liked the strange sights and sounds they brought to Boston.

Then at age nineteen, his father died. Paul took over his business and supported his mother, brothers, and sisters. His work wasn't as fine as that of Apollos Revere, but he had good ideas and lots of energy. His shop did well.

As the years went by, Paul became a husband and the father of eight children. Every Sunday he and his family attended Boston's New Brick Church, where Paul had grown up. When his first wife died, he married a young woman who gave him eight more children. They loved each other very much and worked hard to care for their "little lambs," as Paul called his children.

In spite of this loving care, five of the children died as babies. Paul and Rachel Revere were heartbroken. But Rachel told him, "Keep up your courage and trust yourself and your family into the hands of a good God who will take care of us."

In good times and bad, Paul kept busy. He continued to run his father's metalworking business. Revere also helped Boston get its first streetlights, worked to regulate the city's growing trade, started a fire insurance company and a charitable organization. He always attended town meetings where the people of Boston decided how to run their city. Somehow, he still found time to go horseback riding almost every day.

When England increased the American colonists' taxes, Paul Revere made an important decision. He joined the Sons of Liberty, a group of men who encouraged Americans to seek greater freedom from Britain. One night in 1773, Revere helped dump English tea into the Boston Harbor to protest trade laws.

Paul Revere's house in Boston's North End was built in 1676, and the Revere family moved there in 1770. Part of the road Revere traveled in his midnight ride is now a National Park. On Patriots' Day, April 19, Boston children ring the town bell at midnight and remember the courage of Paul Revere.

The British became more and more worried about their American colonies and patriots like Paul Revere. They sent soldiers to make the people obey English laws, but this only made many Americans more angry. And the Sons of Liberty made things very difficult for the British soldiers.

By 1775, England realized it would have to use force against the American patriots. Paul Revere and his friends knew a fight was coming. "We need a plan to warn people on the other side of the river of a British attack," he told Colonel Conant, a local militia leader. "The sexton [caretaker] at the Old North Church would let us use the steeple to send a signal."

"Splendid idea!" said the Colonel. "That church is tall enough for a light to be seen in Charlestown. But folks will need to know what route the British troops are taking."

"I thought of that already, sir," said Revere with a smile. "If the sol-

diers travel on land, we'll shine one lantern. If they go by boat across the bay and then march northwest, we'll use two lanterns."

They agreed on the signal plan and told the others who needed to know about it. Then they waited.

On April 18, 1775, a boy ran into Revere's shop. "I have important news!" he said breathlessly. "The British soldiers are getting ready to march! I work in the stable where they keep their horses, and I overheard them talking."

"Thank you for coming to me," Revere said. Other reports of military activity kept coming to him. By the end of the day, his friend Dr. Joseph Warren knew the British plan.

"The soldiers have been ordered to arrest Samuel Adams and John Hancock in Lexington," Dr. Warren told Revere. "Then they will go on to Concord and destroy our ammunition. Will you ride to Lexington and Concord with a warning?"

★ ★ ★ ★ ★ ★

We should remember how Revere pictured the cause of American freedom. In a sketch he drew in 1775, he pictured America as a lady praying. Looking up, she said, "Lord, our hope is in You." From Heaven, God's words came down toward America, saying, "I have delivered and I will deliver."

"Of course!" Revere said. "And on the way, I'll stop and tell the men to hang two lanterns in the steeple window."

Revere rowed across the river to Charlestown. Patriots were waiting with a horse that would take him the rest of the way.

British soldiers guarded the roads, but somehow Revere got through. By morning, Samuel Adams and John Hancock had safely escaped from Lexington and the American Minutemen were armed and ready to stop the British.

Soon fighting broke out in other places, and the American Revolutionary War began. Paul Revere joined the army and served as a lieutenant colonel. He also made bullets and cannons for the Americans to use. The first American paper money was designed and printed by him.

When the Revolution ended, Paul Revere went back to his silver shop. "What shall I make now that we don't need cannons and bullets?" he wondered. "I know! I'll make bells." Soon his new foundry was supplying bells to churches throughout New England. Some of them are still ringing today.

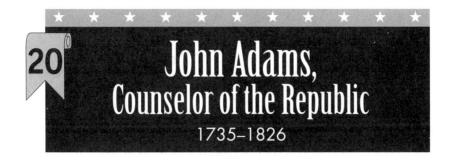

John Adams, Counselor of the Republic
1735–1826

W hy are you are defending those murdering Redcoats?" Samuel Adams
angrily said to his cousin John. "They killed five innocent Americans
and they should pay for it!"

"I don't see why you're so determined to see them hang," John said.
"They would never have shot into the crowd if that mob hadn't refused to
stop throwing rocks and garbage at them. Besides, their commander ordered
them to take aim and fire. A soldier has to obey orders."

Unlike his hot-headed cousin Sam, John Adams was logical and cau-
tious. He hated British oppression, but it made him unhappy when people
called the soldiers' self-defense the "Boston Massacre."

"You know, Sam, facts are stubborn things," John said. "Regardless of
our wishes, we cannot change the facts or the evidence. The law commands
what is good and punishes what is evil in all, whether rich or poor, high or
low. We dare not bend it to suit our opinions or the demands of the people."

Later, John told his wife Abigail about the argument. "I'm afraid my
decision to defend these British soldiers will make me a very unpopular
man."

"Well, dear, I'm proud of you," Abigail said. "You stood up for what
you believe in. I think people will see that and think more highly of you
for it."

Sure enough, the people of Boston realized that John Adams was a
man of courage and honesty. In 1771, they chose him to serve as one of
their lawmakers.

By 1774, John was convinced that the American colonies needed to break away from English rule. But most of the other representatives to the First Continental Congress in Philadelphia weren't ready to consider such a dangerous idea. So John kept quiet and waited for the right time to speak up.

The next year, following the battles of Lexington and Concord, the American Congress met again. John Adams told the other delegates, "It's time we gave up on all these halfway efforts at standing up for our rights," he told the other representatives. "The British intend to force us to bow to their demands. We need more than a few hundred minutemen in each colony in order to resist them. We need a Continental Army!"

★　★　★　★　★　★

John and Abigail Adams were the first to live in our nation's White House. On the fireplace mantel in the dining room, you will see Adams' prayer engraved. He wrote, "I ask heaven to place the best of blessings on this house and all that shall ever live in it. May none but honest and wise men ever rule under this roof."

A gasp of surprise could be heard across the room, but John continued. "If all our troops are organized under one commander—a man like George Washington—we may have a chance of defending our liberty."

After days of talking, the other delegates agreed. Throughout the next few months, John Adams worked extremely hard to make the war with England a success. Many members of Congress still thought America was just standing up for its rights. They expected to continue as part of England. But in September, King George turned down their peace offer.

The coming of 1776 brought increasing support for John Adams' belief in American independence. On June 7, Richard Henry Lee from Virginia stood in Congress and said, "I suggest that we declare these United Colonies free and independent states."

"And I agree!" said John Adams. The members of Congress chose John to help write a Declaration of Independence. He picked Thomas Jefferson to do most of the writing, but when it came time to convince the other delegates to sign the Declaration, John Adams took over.

With his eyes blazing, he said, "Before God, I believe the time for independence has come. My whole heart is in this measure. All that I have, and all that I am, and all that I hope in this life, I am now ready to give for my country. Live or die, I am for the Declaration!"

The next day, Congress voted to accept the Declaration of Independence. John Adams could hardly wait to write and tell his wife. "This will be the most outstanding date in the history of America," he told her. "It ought to be remembered every year with solemn acts of devotion to God Almighty, parades, bells, and fireworks!"

As pleased as he was over the decision, John sometimes felt afraid for America. Always most comfortable writing down his ideas and feelings on paper, he picked up a pen and poured out his heart. "We may plan for liberty, but it is faith in God and morality alone which can make freedom stand securely. The only foundation for a free constitution is pure virtue."

He prayed that the tears, suffering, and death brought to Americans by the War for Independence would turn people's hearts to God.

Many of Adams' thoughts about government were printed and read by leaders in the thirteen colonies. They provided wise direction for the states as they wrote their constitutions. John's own state of Massachusetts asked him to write its constitution. He did the job well, adding a bill of rights that legally protected individual freedoms. Several states used this document as a model, and later it contributed to the creation of the U.S. Constitution and Bill of Rights.

For the rest of his life, John Adams faithfully served his country—as a foreign diplomat, vice president under George Washington, and our second president. When he died on the fiftieth anniversary of the Declaration of Independence, he was looking forward to heaven and a reunion with his wife, Abigail.

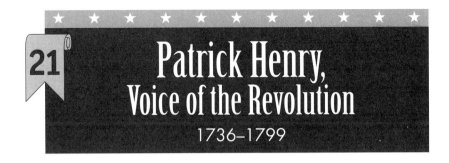

21 Patrick Henry,
Voice of the Revolution
1736–1799

Eleven-year-old Patrick Henry listened closely as the Presbyterian preacher Samuel Davies spoke. The country church was filled with people from all over Hanover County, Virginia, who came to hear the gifted young minister. His strong, pleasant voice and dramatic speaking held Patrick's attention better than his uncle's sermons at the Anglican church.

When the service ended, Patrick followed his mother and sisters out of the church. The family climbed into the buggy and began their ride home.

"Mother, is Reverend Davies the best preacher you've ever heard?" Patrick asked.

"Folks say the only man better is Rev. George Whitefield," his mother said. "We're blessed to have a preacher like Samuel Davies." Her hands firmly on the horses' reins, she said, "Now tell me, what did you learn today?"

As he did every Sunday, young Henry repeated the main Bible verses Rev. Davies had used. Then, using his best voice, he recited as much of the sermon as he could remember.

"Well done, Patrick!" his mother. "You have a good memory and a nice way with words. Maybe you'll be a preacher when you grow up."

In 1764, Patrick Henry was elected to the Virginia House of Burgesses. The wealthy and well-educated men from coastal Virginia didn't pay much attention to the tall, thin lawyer from Hanover County—until he began to speak about things he deeply believed. Some of Patrick Henry's best speeches were about American's rights and England's wrongs.

In 1774, the House of Burgesses decided it was time for all the colonies to send representatives to an annual Congress. They chose Henry as one of their delegates to the first Continental Congress in Philadelphia later that year.

The following spring, the Virginia House of Burgesses tried to meet as usual at Williamsburg. But the Royal Governor dismissed them as punishment for their defiance of the king and parliament.

"He won't get rid of us that easily!" said the fiery young Thomas Jefferson. He and the other Burgesses agreed to meet at St. John's Anglican Church in Richmond.

In late March, 120 of Virginia's greatest men crowded into the church. Among them were George Washington, Thomas Jefferson, Richard Henry Lee, Rev. Peter Muhlenberg, and Patrick Henry.

On the fourth day, conservative members began to talk about their hope for peace with England. "The only way we can return to the happy days we once enjoyed is to appeal to King George," one of the men said.

Patrick Henry stood to speak. He read two important resolutions— actions he wanted Virginia to take immediately. "Instead of paying taxes for British troops to come and watch over us, we need a trained militia to defend us," he said. "This colony should be immediately put into a state of defense and a large number of men trained and armed for that purpose."

"You make it sound like we're already at war with our mother country," said one of the delegates. "Don't you think this is a little premature?"

Henry answered respectfully, "It is natural to shut our eyes against a painful truth. But I am willing to know the whole truth and act as it demands."

He looked at those who had spoken strongly for peace and said, "Ask yourself why our petitions to England have been answered with British soldiers on our land and sea. Has Great Britain any enemy in this part of the world? No sir, she has none. These troops are meant for us. They've been sent

to fasten upon us chains which the British have been so long making."

As Henry talked, his eyes blazed and his voice became louder. "We have tried arguing with them for ten years. We have done everything that could be done to turn away the storm which is now coming on. There is no longer any room for hope. If we wish to save the rights that are ours by law, we must fight!"

He continued with even more force, "They tell us that we are weak—unable to face so strong an opponent. But when will we be stronger?" He paused to let his words sink in. "We are not weak if we make use of the means God has placed in our power. Three million people, armed in the holy cause of liberty, and in such a country as we possess, are invincible against any force," he reasoned. "Besides, we will not fight our battles alone. There is a just God who rules over the nations. He will raise up friends to fight for us."

> "Whether American independence will be a blessing or a curse depends on how our people make use of what God has given us. If they are wise, they will be great and happy. If they are not, they will be miserable. Righteousness alone can exalt a nation (Proverbs 14:34). Reader! Whoever you are, remember this, and in your world practice goodness and encourage it in others."
> —Patrick Henry

The room was warm and a crowd had gathered around the open church windows to hear what was happening. Henry concluded his speech with words from the Bible. "Gentlemen may cry, peace, peace—but there is no peace . . . Is life so dear, or peace so sweet, that we would purchase it at the price of chains and slavery? God forbid it! I know not what course others may take; but as for me, give me liberty or give me death!"

When the House of Burgesses voted, Henry's resolution won by five votes. Then he and others created a plan for organizing the Virginia militia. It was accepted and Henry became the colony's military commander.

In 1776, Patrick Henry resigned his military position to become governor of the newly created state of Virginia. For the rest of his life, he remained concerned about the rights of common people. He deserves much of the credit for the addition of the Bill of Rights to our U.S. Constitution.

22 John Peter Gabriel Muhlenberg, Fighting Parson
1746–1807

Peter Muhlenberg tossed and turned in his bed. Sleep would not come. *I am a pastor, not a patriot soldier!* he told himself. But the words of Patrick Henry's speech before the Virginia House of Burgesses [colonial legislature] kept repeating in his mind.

Henry had said, "Gentlemen may cry, peace, peace—but there is no peace. The war is actually begun! Is life so valuable, or peace so sweet, as to be purchased at the price of chains and slavery? Forbid it, Almighty God! I know not what course others may take; but as for me . . . give me liberty or give me death!"

Then Parson Muhlenberg thought about fellow Virginian George Washington's request. "Muhlenberg, we need you in the Continental Army. You are a man other men will gladly follow. Will you consider organizing a regiment of German-Americans for the cause of liberty?"

I can't put the decision off any longer, Muhlenberg thought. "God please help me make the right choice," he prayed.

The next Sunday morning, Parson Muhlenberg stood before the Woodstock Lutheran congregation. He looked fondly at the people he had pastored for five years. He had performed their weddings, baptized their babies, and buried their dead. Many of them had become special friends. *What will America's liberty cost them?* he wondered.

With a heavy heart, Muhlenberg began his sermon. "I am preaching today from the third chapter of Ecclesiastes," he told the people. "'There is a time for everything, and a season for every activity under heaven: a time

to be born and a time to die . . . a time to kill and a time to heal . . . a time for war and a time for peace.'"

The people that filled the church to hear his wonderful preaching listened quietly. They knew their pastor believed America should be free from England. Most of them strongly agreed that it was time for war.

When Parson Muhlenberg reached the end of his sermon, he said, "There is a time to pray and a time to fight. This is the time to fight!" Then he took off his minister's robe. "Oh!" the people gasped in surprise. There stood Muhlenberg in a Continental Army officer's uniform!

"I must tell you good-bye," he said solemnly. "I am needed in the fight for independence. Perhaps some of you will join me."

Men began standing all over the church. "I will go!" one said. "Count me in too!" said another.

Soon the fighting parson had his regiment of brave Virginians.

After two years of military service under George Washington, Muhlenberg was made a Brigadier General. In 1779, he took command of all the Virginia troops. His leadership helped force the British General Cornwallis to surrender in 1781.

> ★ ★ ★ ★ ★ ★
>
> When you visit Statuary Hall in the U.S. Capitol Building, be sure to look for Peter Muhlenberg. The artist depicted him taking off his minister's robes to reveal the military uniform underneath. In 1889, the State of Pennsylvania placed his statue there as a reminder of his willingness to give his life for freedom.

When the war ended in 1783, Muhlenberg returned to his home state of Pennsylvania. There he served as the state vice president under Benjamin Franklin. He also represented Pennsylvania in three sessions of the Continental Congress. He spent the rest of his life faithfully serving the young nation he had fought to create.

23 George Washington, Father of America
1732–1799

We must make it clear to the French that England will not tolerate invasion of its territory," Governor Dinwiddie told the Virginia officers. "I need a volunteer to carry my warning to the French commander at Fort Le Boeuf." He looked around the circle of men. "This will be a dangerous mission. Anyone who takes it will face a rugged wilderness, Indians, and wild animals. And the winter weather will make traveling on horseback difficult."

Young Major George Washington spoke up. "Five years ago I went into the frontier, so I know the risks. But I will count it an honor to take your message to the French, Governor."

In late 1753, Washington left the comforts of colonial Virginia and headed toward the wilderness of western Pennsylvania. All he had to guide him was a compass and his earlier experience as a surveyor. As he traveled, he drew a map for Dinwiddie. It showed his path through the thick snowy forests, across icy rivers, and over high mountains.

Washington looked with amazement at the awesome land that stretched out before him. *No wonder the French want America for themselves!* he thought. *They will never agree to let it go to the English peacefully.* With the thought of war in mind, Washington carefully marked on his map all the French forts he found along the way.

After twenty-six days, George reached Fort Le Boeuf. As soon as the French wrote their answer, he started back to Williamsburg. After nearly freezing in the cruel winter wilderness, he handed Governor Dinwiddie the message that started a war.

"Washington, you look like death!" Dinwiddie said when he saw the young officer again.

"But I am not dead, sir," Washington answered. "Providence has chosen to save my life."

During the war with France, Washington risked his life many times. After one of the worst battles, he said in a letter to his brother: "Dear Jack, I am writing to assure you that I am still alive by the miraculous care of Providence that protected me beyond all human expectation. I had four bullets through my coat, and two horses shot from under me. Yet I escaped unhurt."

Over twenty years later, when America declared its independence from England, George Washington again faced great danger and hardship. By then, his courageous military service had earned him the rank of colonel. Many people believed he should be placed in charge of the entire American army.

The Continental Congress discussed whom to choose as army commander. While they debated and disagreed, Washington walked the streets of Philadelphia or paced in his room. *I will not be chosen*, he thought. *It is too much responsibility, too high an honor. And the cause of freedom is so doubtful.*

In spite of his worries, the delegates decided he was the best choice. "Congratulations, General," they said as they shook his hand. With tears in his eyes, Washington told his friend Patrick Henry, "I don't have the training for such an important command." But the delegates stood firm in their decision. At dinner, they saluted him and solemn silence filled the dining room.

"The sword of liberty has been put in your hands, General Washington," a delegate said. "Your country has chosen you."

The outcome of the war showed that George Washington was a good choice. But he didn't take credit for America's victory. "The hand of Providence has been so clear in the course of the war," Washington wrote in a letter to another general. "A man would have to be worse than an atheist not to gratefully admit God's help."

After the United States won its independence from England, it again chose Washington for a position of great honor and responsibility. In 1789, he became the nation's first president.

When America's great war hero arrived in New York (then the U.S. Capital) for his inauguration, the entire city was decorated. As he rode down the street, people tossed flowers down on his carriage like confetti.

At nine o'clock in the morning on April 30, all the church bells in the city called people to come and pray for their new president.

★ ★ ★ ★ ★ ★

The Washington Monument is over 555 feet tall, and at its top is a metal cap that reads, "Praise be to God." Those words seem to fit the great commander who trusted in Providence.

Then, around noon, Washington traveled in a parade to the Federal State House. Inside, everything was ready for him to take his oath of office.

President Washington looked handsome in his dark brown suit, his silver sword by his side. He laid his hand on the Bible, which the Secretary of the Senate held on a red velvet cushion, and promised to serve his country faithfully. At the end, Washington solemnly added four words to the required oath. "So help me, God," he said and his voice trembled with strong feeling.

After the Inauguration, Washington, his vice-president John Adams, and all of Congress went to St. Paul's Chapel for a special church service.

Throughout his presidency, George Washington looked to heaven for help and approval. "It is the duty of all nations to acknowledge the providence of Almighty God," he said in his Thanksgiving Proclamation, "to obey His will, to be grateful for His benefits, and humbly ask His protection and kindness."

24

Benjamin Rush,
Doctor of Hearts and Minds
1747–1813

Dr. Benjamin Rush enjoyed people, and he liked to talk. His enthusiastic voice and strong ideas could be heard each day in his busy Philadelphia medical office. He also liked to pass on his knowledge of science and medecine to college students.

But the most interesting talks he had were with fellow members of the American Philosophical Society. This group, started by Benjamin Franklin, discussed scientific discoveries, great books and ideas, religion, and current events.

One evening, Dr. Rush and the other men listened closely as a new-comer joined in the discussion. "I don't understand why the American colonies allow England to keep using them," said Thomas Paine.

"But surely as an Englishman, you have some loyalty to our mother country," said one of the men seated nearby.

"Like most of the world, England is full of oppression," Paine said. "I prefer to be counted as a Son of Liberty."

"Well, you're in good company here," said Dr. Rush warmly. "Most of us are firm believers in American independence."

"As you should be," Paine replied. "The colonies are too far from England to enjoy an equal share in its business and government. Common sense should tell you that the English only want the colonies for their own profit, not yours."

"Hmm . . . common sense," thought Dr. Rush aloud. "Paine, you should put these ideas of yours into a pamphlet. I suggest you call it

Common Sense." He raised his hand to silence Paine's protest. "No, I'm serious. And I'll prove it by helping you pay for the printing."

Around the time of Benjamin Rush's thirtieth birthday, Paine's essay was published. Thanks to Dr. Rush and others, about 500,000 copies were printed. Soon people throughout the colonies were reading it and talking about what good sense it made.

Six months later, in July of 1776, the majority of Americans welcomed the Declaration of Independence. Dr. Benjamin Rush, a Pennsylvania delegate to the Continental Congress, eagerly signed it and encouraged everyone he knew to support the fight for American independence. During the Congress, he became friends with Thomas Jefferson, John Adams, and other great patriots. These friendships lasted the rest of his life.

Dr. Benjamin Rush worked for many years at Pennsylvania Hospital in Philadelphia. Started in 1751, it is America's oldest hospital and it still takes care of sick people today.

Dr. Rush joined the Continental Army and was chosen as a surgeon general. But his strong opinions about how things should be done, and his hot temper, got him in trouble. So he returned to teaching medicine and doctoring the people of Philadelphia.

While Rush often got into arguments with other doctors, his students loved him and his classes became very popular. When Rush was a young man, he and other Americans had to go to Scotland, England, and Europe to study medicine. But in the late 1700s, Dr. Rush's reputation began to attract students from those countries to the University of Pennsylvania. Soon the city of Philadelphia became the world's leading medical center.

Dr. Rush was also popular with the many poor patients who received medical care from him without any charge. His compassion for the needy caused him to start America's first free clinic in 1786. Rush believed Americans would lead healthier lives if they gave up coffee, tea, liquor, and tobacco, and exercised regularly. Over the years, he became increasingly interested in understanding and caring for the mentally ill.

As a devoted Christian, he took very seriously Jesus' command to love

others as Christ loved each of us. This concern for others included the African American people. Early in his career, Dr. Rush wrote an essay against slavery. Some of his patients quit seeing him because of this, but many others came to take their place in his office. In 1787, Rush started the Pennsylvania Society for Promoting Abolition—the first American group of its kind.

Always eager to improve the lives of Americans, he encouraged several changes in education. "We're spending too much time on subjects like Latin and Greek," he argued. "Our children need more practical subjects like science." Rush thought girls as well as boys should receive a well-rounded education. He also believed the Bible deserved a place of honor in every classroom.

"The Bible contains more essential knowledge than any other book in the world," Dr. Rush wrote. "I believe everyone who received early instruction in the Bible has been made wiser and better by its influence on his mind."

Rush is buried in the cemetery at Philadelphia's Christ Church, but his influence lives on in Christians who work to make their country a better place. The name Philadelphia means "brotherly love," and Dr. Rush was a wonderful example of that principle to his city, and to us.

Rush thought about the many Americans who had no respect for the law or the rights of others. He suggested an answer to the problem of crime. "It is sad that we waste so much time and money in punishing crimes and make so little effort to prevent them," he wrote. "The education of our youth in the principles of Christianity by means of the Bible will teach them belief in the equality of everyone, respect for fair laws, and virtues that support democracy."

John Jay, International Peacemaker
1745-1829

25

After three years of hard work to help New York become a strong state, John Jay felt ready for some new and different challenges. He looked out the carriage window in amazement at how Philadelphia had grown since he last served in the Congress.

"Welcome back, Jay!" John Adams said as the New York delegate entered Philadelphia's State House. "It's good to have you back, but I'm afraid this session of Congress will be anything but pleasant."

It didn't take long for Jay to see how angry some of the state delegates were with each other. And the hothead Henry Laurens wasn't helping matters either. Soon the Congressmen called for his resignation as President of the assembly.

"We need someone with a level head in charge of these sessions," Franklin said. "How about John Jay?"

"Great idea!" said a delegate nearby. "Yes, Jay is a man of great personal character and experience," said another. A vote was taken, and Jay became President of the quarreling Congress.

For the next nine months, John Jay tried to help the delegates work through their problems for the good of their new nation. It was a very difficult and frustrating job.

In spite of the problems, Jay didn't give up. Instead, he encouraged Congress to create a stronger national government. He also pointed out a major problem for America—its debts. With the fight for independence going on so many years and costing so much, the United States had

borrowed money from other countries and from many of its wealthy citizens.

"Let it never be said that as soon as America became independent, she also became bankrupt," Jay warned the delegates. "When all the nations of the earth are admiring this infant nation's courage and achievements, we dare not let broken promises destroy its reputation and respect."

When his work in Congress ended, Jay received another difficult assignment. He had proved that he could stand up under tremendous pressure, so the congressional delegates chose him as America's representative to Spain. They needed someone calm and clear-thinking to convince Spain that it should support the United States in its struggle for independence.

★ ★ ★ ★ ★ ★

If you could talk to John Jay, he would probably tell you the same thing he told his children: "You have the Book." He believed the Bible held the answers to all of life's big questions. The American Bible Society (ABS) is still carrying out Jay's dream of providing people around the world with the Bible. It even makes the Bible available in the Braille System and American Sign Language. The American Bible Society makes its home in New York City— John Jay's hometown.

For two long and lonely years, Jay did his best, but Spain couldn't be budged.

Then, something wonderful happened. America's military victories made it clear England would have to admit defeat. The war for independence had been won. Now, it was time for the United States and Great Britain to make a peace treaty.

The negotiations began in Paris in the summer of 1782. John Jay and his good friend Dr. Benjamin Franklin began the talks, and John Adams joined them later.

Since France and Spain also had claims on America, they had to be included in the talks.

After his meeting with the Spanish negotiator, Jay reported to Franklin. "Spain wants to set our boundary at the Appalachian Mountains and refuses to let us sail the Mississippi River," Jay told Franklin.

"Well, we can count of France's help," Franklin said. "They have never failed us in the past."

When the French negotiators saw how much land America wanted to claim, they said, "You are asking too much!" They also didn't like the idea of the American colonies uniting in one large new nation.

When the two American negotiators were alone, Franklin said, "If we cannot depend on France, who can we depend on?"

"Only upon God and ourselves," Jay answered.

Jay's dependence on Divine help must have worked because he soon found a way to negotiate directly with the British. The United States came out a winner, and John Jay received much of the credit.

For the rest of his life, Jay faithfully served his country. His roles included Secretary of Foreign Affairs, a key person in the creation of the U.S. Constitution, the nation's first Chief Justice, negotiator for the Jay Treaty with England (which prevented another war), and then as Governor of New York.

John Jay's Christian faith gave him the courage to make unpopular decisions and to take a personal stand for the truth. After he retired, he spent most of his time in Christian activities. He served as president of the American Bible Society, an organization founded by his son to encourage Bible reading and distribution. Throughout his life, he opposed slavery and believed the United States would have to reject it in order to fulfill God's purpose for this nation.

On America's 50th birthday, Jay made it clear that he knew where the real credit for her victory belonged. "I hope that the peace, happiness, and prosperity enjoyed by our country will cause those in government to recommend a general and public return of praise to God from whose goodness these blessings come."

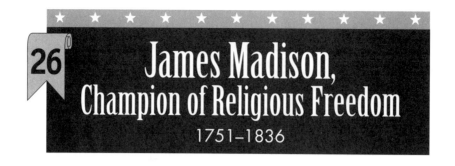

26 James Madison, Champion of Religious Freedom
1751–1836

James Madison listened closely as his tutor, Reverend Thomas Martin, talked about which college he should attend. "I know most young men of well-to-do Virginia families choose William and Mary," Martin said, "but I sincerely hope you won't."

"Wait! Don't tell me. Let me guess. You want me to enroll in the College of New Jersey [Princeton]," James said teasingly.

Martin smiled. "Yes, but it's not just because it's where I attended. I truly believe the school has better teachers, and there's your health to think of," the minister said. "You need to get away from Virginia's Tidewater [marshy coastal area] and it's sicknesses."

Madison agreed, and so he began his college studies in New Jersey at the age of nineteen. He had many outstanding teachers, especially John Witherspoon, the college president. Unlike Madison, who had been raised in the Anglican church, most of his teachers were Presbyterians. Many of them had been part of the Great Awakening. They encouraged their students to think for themselves, to love liberty, and to practice common sense.

James studied hard and graduated in three years. Since he hadn't decided whether to become a minister or an attorney, he went on studying Hebrew, the Bible, theology, and law after he returned to Montpelier, his family's home in Virginia. Although he often heard talk of America's struggle with England and the problems of taxation, he was much more interested in how government worked and in the freedom of religion.

One day James went with his father to the nearby town of Orange.

While walking down the street, he heard a voice shouting from the window of the jail.

"These are a strange sort of prisoners you're holding behind bars," Madison said to a man outside the jail. "Who are they and what are the charges against them?"

"Oh, it's just a bunch of Baptist preachers," the man told him. "They know it's against the law to hold meetings or pass out sermons on paper, but they do it anyway."

"But for the most part, Baptists believe the same as any other Christians," Madison said. "Why shouldn't they be free to practice their beliefs?"

"Perhaps you've forgotten, young man," said a gentleman nearby, "ever since its founding Virginia has been faithful to the Anglican Church."

"Even if it's priests are becoming lazy, proud, and dishonest?" young Madison asked angrily. "And the people aren't becoming better citizens by being forced to support them. If anything, they're getting worse!"

When Madison returned home, he wrote to one of his college friends about his frustration with Virginia's laws. "I want to breathe your free air," he told his Philadelphia friend. "Here in Virginia, where the Anglican Church is established as the only true form of worship, the result is ignorance, slavery, corruption, and persecution."

Out of concern for those whose rights were being violated by government-enforced religion, Madison decided to become active in Virginia politics. In 1776, he helped write Virginia's first state constitution and its

★ ★ ★ ★ ★ ★

Although James Madison defended the rights of all religious groups, he continued to attend the Anglican (eventually called Episcopal in America) church. During his years as president, St. John's Episcopal Church was built in Washington, D.C. and is located one block north of the White House. This beautiful building soon became known as the "Church of the Presidents." Madison picked pew Number 28 (now 54) and the next five presidents sat there. That pew is now set aside for any President who attends services. If you visit the church, be sure to look for the prayer book signed by many of our nation's leaders.

declaration of rights.

While serving in the Virginia legislature, he met someone who shared many of his ideas about religious freedom. "Jefferson, let me tell you what I think," Madison said to his new friend. "Religious bondage limits and weakens the mind, and makes it unfit for every worthwhile effort and every expanded outlook."

"I think you're right," said Jefferson. "So we had better do our best to convince people that government shouldn't try to control religion."

In 1785, Madison wrote a paper on religious freedom. He tried to carefully explain why he disapproved of a state religion. His argument made such good sense that many Virginians took his side. But other leaders like Patrick Henry disagreed.

Madison kept speaking up for religious freedom. He also became a supporter of a stronger federal government and helped create the U.S. Constitution when he was just thirty-six years old. Two years later, he used his influence in securing a Bill of Rights. He made sure freedom of religion was included in this important new document.

In 1809, James Madison became President. Under his leadership, the United States came through a second war with England, developed a stronger federal government, and began its development as a world power. His guiding principle throughout his life is stated in these words: "Religion, or the duty we owe to our Creator . . . can only be directed by thought and belief, not by force or violence. . . It is the shared duty of everyone to practice Christian mercy and love towards each other."

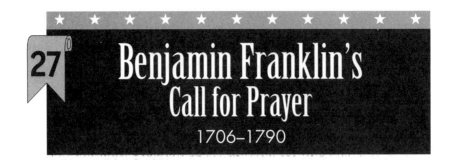

Benjamin Franklin's
Call for Prayer
1706–1790

Benjamin Franklin groaned as he dressed for another day of debate in the Constitutional Convention. "My mind is ready," he said to his servant, "but this eighty-year-old body it lives in gives me considerable pain."

While he continued his preparations, Franklin repeated his usual morning prayer. "Oh, Bountiful Father! Give me greater wisdom in knowing what is best for me. Strengthen my determination to do what that wisdom demands."

After dressing and eating breakfast, Franklin went by carriage to Independence Hall, meeting place of the Constitutional Convention. Many people waved to him, and he called friendly greetings in return. Philadelphia respected and loved Ben Franklin for his generous, kindhearted ways, his keen sense of humor, and his great intelligence. Most Americans thought their new nation was fortunate to have such a wise man helping to create its government. But few of them understood what hard work it was for Franklin and the other members of Congress.

As the hours passed on June 28, 1787, the meeting room grew hot from the weather outside and from the angry debate inside. The delegates couldn't agree on how to design a government that would fairly represent individual states. The representatives from small states worried that larger states would have more power. Those from large states argued that they had a right to greater voice in government, since they had more people.

Bitter and unkind words flew back and forth across the room. Some men became so mad they stormed out of the assembly. Rather than binding

the thirteen colonies together, it seemed the Convention was about to tear the new nation apart.

Then Benjamin Franklin, leader of Pennsylvania and host of the Convention, stood to speak. "The small progress we have made after four or five weeks of intense work, and our different opinion on almost every question, is a sad proof of the shortcomings of human understanding.

"We have seen our lack of political wisdom, since we have been running around in search of it. We have looked to ancient history for models of government and been reminded of how those governments dissolved. And we have considered the modern states of Europe, but none of their constitutions are right for our nation.

"Since we are in the dark, how has it happened that we have not once thought of humbly asking the Father of lights to illuminate our understanding?"

The men in the room had grown quiet and sad as Franklin spoke. When he talked about the lack of prayer, some of them looked down in shame. But young Alexander Hamilton jokingly said, "I don't see the need to call in foreign-aid."

> ★ ★ ★ ★ ★ ★
> In 1954 the Congress decided to create a Prayer Room in our nation's capitol. You will find it on the west side of the Rotunda. It contains an altar and an open Bible, and its stained glass window pictures George Washington in prayer along with the words of Psalm 16:1.

Franklin ignored the comment and continued speaking. "At the beginning of our war with Great Britain, when we were most aware of danger, we had daily prayer in this room for God's protection. Our prayers were answered. It is God who made it possible for us to meet together now in peace and plan for the future. Have we now forgotten that powerful Friend? Do we think we no longer need His help?

"I have lived a long time, and the longer I live, the more convincing proofs I see of this truth—God rules in the affairs of men. And if a sparrow cannot fall to the ground without His notice, is it probable that an empire can rise without His aid?

"We have been assured in the Bible, 'Except the Lord build the house, they labor in vain who build it.' So, I ask that from now on prayers asking God's help and blessing on our meetings be held every morning before we begin our business."

Then Dr. Franklin sat down. James Madison, president of the Convention, immediately agreed with his request for prayer. Roger Sherman also spoke up for the idea.

"Gentlemen, if we do take this action, the public will think things are going badly and we are getting desperate," said young Alexander Hamilton.

A North Carolina delegate added, "We don't have the money to pay a minister to lead us in prayer every day."

Next, Edmund Randolph of Virginia spoke. "Perhaps instead we could invite a minister to preach to us on the Fourth of July."

Everyone seemed to agree. So, on the anniversary of America's Declaration of Independence, the convention delegates gathered in a local church.

Each day of business in Congress begins with prayers led by the Senate Chaplain and the House Chaplain. These prayers are also printed in the Congressional Record, a written account of each day's business.

After preaching, Reverend William Rogers prayed for the success of the Constitutional Convention. "We ask You, heavenly Father, to bless these delegates day by day with Your inspiring presence. Be their wisdom and strength. Help them heal all divisions so that the United States of America may form one example of a free and excellent government."

Soon after Dr. Franklin's reminder of the need for God's help, the unfriendly attitude of the men changed. They began to work together for the good of the country, and they created a strong government that is still working for us today.

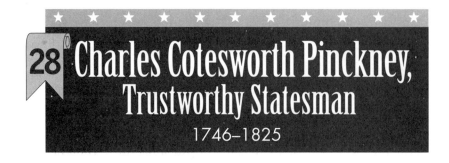

President John Adams shook hands with General Pinckney and motioned for him to take a seat. "Thank you for coming," the President said. "You served your country well during our War for Independence and now America desperately needs you to help us make peace with France."

"Thank you for your confidence in me, Mr. President," Pinckney said. "I understand that France's attacks on our ships are becoming more frequent. This could lead to war."

"Yes, but I think we can prevent it," said President Adams. "That's why I'm asking you, John Marshall of Virginia, and Elbridge Gerry of Massachusetts, to talk with France's foreign minister, Talleyrand."

In October 1797, Marshall, Pinckney, and Gerry reached Paris. Soon after they arrived, Talleyrand sent three secret agents to talk with them.

"Our government will be glad to discuss how we can stop attacks on American ships," one of the Frenchmen said. "But first, you must agree to one thing."

"And what is that, sir?" Pinckney said politely. He carefully hid his worried feelings and his fear that Talleyrand was up to some trick.

Another of the French agents spoke up, "We will require the United States to make a loan to our government." Before the Americans could answer, he continued. "And Monsieur Talleyrand requires a gift of $250,000."

The American diplomats looked at one another in shock. Then Pinckney spoke up. "No, sir. It is no, no—not a sixpence!"

When the French agents were gone, Pinckney, Marshall, and Gerry let the President Adams know what had happened. Upon hearing that the French had asked for a bribe, the President told Congress in a private meeting. The Congressmen agreed that the U.S. negotiators should come home immediately.

Meanwhile, the newspapers found out what had happened. The only thing still secret was the names of the three Frenchmen, so they were called X, Y, and Z. Soon everyone was talking about the X, Y, Z Affair, and war with France seemed likely.

Pinckney returned to active military duty as major general of the American soldiers in the South. He served his country faithfully until the danger of war was passed in 1800. Because of the X, Y, Z Affair, the United States Congress created a Navy, and the nation became respected for its honesty and its growing military strength.

After running for vice president and president, Pinckney went back to his work as an attorney in Charleston. He also helped many good causes, including the Charleston Bible Society. This organization, which met at Pinckney's house for fifteen years, gave Bibles to African Americans and taught them how to read. Pinckney was also faithful in serving in the Episcopal church.

When Pinckney was still a young man, his father wrote these words about him: "I hope he will have the blessings of God and deserve the friendship of all good men. I expect him to use all his abilities in serving God, his country, the cause of religious and civil liberty, and in supporting justice between men. I hope he will never dishonor himself or his profession by ever appearing disrespectful of God, doing wrong, or supporting oppression of any kind." His father's dream came true.

29 Abigail Adams,
First Lady of Faith
1744–1814

Abigail Adams shook her head sadly as she read a newspaper article about the French Revolution. "John, what will become of France?" she asked her husband. "Is it really true that the priests are being killed and the churches are being closed?"

The Vice President, John Adams, returned his wife's worried look. "Yes, I'm afraid it's all true. Jefferson thinks the French are simply overthrowing tyrants as we Americans did. But I see very little alike between the two."

"I couldn't agree more," Abigail said. "During our struggle for independence from England, we found great strength and support from our ministers and churches. All we have seen in the past makes me believe in the importance of true religion." John nodded in agreement and Abigail continued. "I think it is the only thing that binds people together and gives them a sense of responsibility toward their Maker."

"And of all the religions, Christianity is by far the best," John said. "It is a religion of wisdom, clean living, fairness, and kindness."

> You can visit two of the Adams' family homes in Quincy, Massachusetts (near Boston). During the Revolutionary War, Abigail and the children were often there alone with the fighting nearby. Each morning they prayed together.

Abigail and John Adams shared a deep personal faith in God, and they did their best to pass it on to their nation and family. They felt sad as they watched many of their friends in government turn from firm belief in the Bible. They worried that the French ideas of freedom without obedience to God would take hold in the United States.

When John decided he could best serve his country as President, Abigail supported his decision. She was too sick to be beside him when he won the election, so she did what she had done during the many times they had been apart—she wrote him a letter and prayed for him.

"I don't feel proud today," Abigail wrote. "Instead, I feel a deep awareness of the trust that has been placed in you, and the duties that go with it. You are now the head of a nation."

Talking to God came naturally to Abigail. She included a prayer in her letter. "O Lord, You have made Your servant ruler over the people. Give him an understanding heart to judge between good and bad." After this prayer from the Bible (1 Kings 3:9), she added her own prayer. "Though I am absent, I am asking that the things that make for peace will not be hidden from you" (Luke 19:42). Then she promised to pray for John's work as President every day.

Abigail laid down her quill pen, salted the page to keep the ink from smearing, and sealed her letter shut with hot wax. *Since I cannot be with John right now, what else can I do to help my country?* she wondered. A wonderful idea popped into her mind. "I know! I will see that our black servant boys get an education."

After watching the Battle of Bunker Hill and learning a best friend had been killed, Abigail wrote John, "God gives strength and power to His people. He is a refuge for us."

Right away, Abigail enrolled the boys in a local school. Some of her neighbors didn't like that at all. But Abigail said, "They are as free as any of the young men. Just because their faces are black, will we deny them the right to learn?" Her eyes flashed with anger. "Is this the Christian principle of doing to others as we would have others do to us? I'm not ashamed that I've taught the boys to read and write in my living room. I hope we will all go to heaven together."

Abigail's courage and strong beliefs made her a wonderful advisor to John. "Come as soon as you can," he wrote to her. "I need your help."

For fifty-four years, Abigail and John Adams were partners in building a strong America. Their son, John Quincy Adams, followed in their footsteps, all the way to the White House.

John Marshall, Great Chief Justice
1755–1835

John Marshall carefully straightened his black robe and prepared to enter the Supreme Court room. In the quietness of his private office, he thought about how to handle the case he must judge. *This is definitely the most difficult and important decision I've had to make since becoming Chief Justice,* he thought. *It will prove whether the Supreme Court has the power to set aside an act [law] of Congress when that act disagrees with the Constitution.*

The past two years hadn't been easy for Chief Justice Marshall. He had been asked by President John Adams to take the job because Adams knew Marshall believed strongly in the power of the federal government. In 1801 when Marshall started to serve, no one took the Supreme Court very seriously. Little by little, he was teaching people that the Court had authority to settle the biggest arguments in America. *But can it really stand up to the U.S. Congress?* he wondered. *It must when the Congress or any state makes laws that are unconstitutional.* he thought. *Otherwise, the U.S. Constitution, created to make us a strong and united nation, will be worthless.*

In the case called *Marbury versus Madison*, Chief Justice Marshall decided Congress was wrong. This took great courage. Other judges followed his example. From then on, everyone knew that when it came to deciding what was legal and what wasn't, the Supreme Court was the highest power.

During his thirty-four years as Chief Justice, Marshall had to make many other difficult decisions. One was whether Congress could start a U. S. bank. The Constitution didn't say anything about it, one way or the other. Again, Marshall thought hard about what was right. When it was time to

give his answer he said, "As long as it is something the United States government actually needs and isn't forbidden by the Constitution, it is legal."

Sometimes the Supreme Court had to solve problems involving religion. Marshall knew that in most American towns, churches helped knit people together and supported good government. In a letter to Reverend Jasper Adams, Marshall said, "Since America is known as a nation of Christians, it would be very strange if our institutions didn't refer to Christianity and show our connection with it. When making decisions about these matters, the Court must be very careful to respect both our religion [Christianity] and each person's right to act on his own beliefs [freedom of conscience]."

Chief Justice John Marshall and the other Supreme Court judges weren't alone in their respect for the U.S. Constitution. Ever since our nation's beginning, Americans have treasured it as our most important document, along with the Bill of Rights, and the Declaration of Independence. These papers have been carefully protected. They are on display in Exhibition Hall at the National Archives Building in Washington, D.C.

As long as John Adams was President, Marshall could count on support from the White House. But later presidents thought the Chief Justice made too many decisions in favor of federal [national], rather than state government. Still, Marshall didn't budge from what he believed. And even those who disagreed with him liked him because of his honesty, intelligence, and pleasant ways.

One day as John Marshall drove along a Virginia road in his horse and buggy, the buggy broke down. Marshall managed to get to a nearby hotel. No one took much notice of the old man in sloppy clothes when he went inside the dining room and ordered some food.

While he ate, he listened to several young men discussing the Christian religion. The talk continued, hour after hour. Finally, one of the men turned to him and said, "Well, my old gentleman, what do you think?"

For the next hour, Marshall talked about the teachings of Jesus. He gave good answers to all the arguments against Christianity.

"He must be a preacher," said one of the fellows to his friends. Marshall smiled and said good-bye. The next day the newspaper told the story of how the Chief Justice spoke up for Christ.

Francis Scott Key, Patriotic Poet
1779–1843

The War of 1812

Y ou may speak with the President now, Mr. Key," said the aide. He then directed the distinguished but worried-looking attorney into President Madison's temporary office—a room in the home of Mrs. Madison's sister.

Key thought, *How tired and sad the President looks*. In his mind he pictured the beautiful White House blackened by flames after the British attack on Washington, D.C. It was a great loss for the nation and for the Madisons. The President's voice brought him back to the present.

"It's good to see you, Key," said the President. "Although I understand you come on a sad mission."

"Yes, sir. Our friend Dr. William Beanes was taken prisoner when the British raided Washington," Francis Key said. "I am certain he is being held in one of the British ships here in the Baltimore Harbor. I have come in hopes of negotiating his release. With your permission, sir."

"Of course, Key, see what you can do," said President Madison. "With England attacking our shores, we may have great need of our doctors."

"Thank you very much, Mr. President," said Key. Then he hurried to talk with the officers in charge of prisoner exchanges.

On September 2, 1814, Key got on board a U.S. diplomatic ship. He paced the deck as the *Minden* sailed toward the floating prison where Dr. Beanes was being held. He felt anxious about his friend, and about his country. In his mind, he could see horrible pictures of the night when the British had burned the Capitol Building and the White House. *What will they*

do next? he wondered. *Are we strong enough to withstand the English forces?*

As the *Minden* neared a British frigate, Key waved a white truce flag. When the ships were alongside, several British officers and soldiers came on board. Key stepped forward and said, "I am here to secure the release of Dr. William Beanes, a U.S. citizen you are illegally holding."

The Englishmen looked at each other and laughed. "I'm afraid that will have to wait a while," said one of them. "We have more important business right now. And since we can't afford to have you tell the troops at Fort McHenry that we're about to fire on them, you'll have to stay here over night." The British soldiers laughed and begin rounding up the *Minden*'s crew and passengers at gun point.

Not long after Key and the other Americans boarded the British warship, it began to fire on Fort McHenry. The canons boomed, and the rockets blazed toward the American fortress. Meanwhile, all Key could do was watch in horror.

When night came, most of the weary and frightened Americans went below deck. All except Key. He couldn't seem to take his eyes off of the battle. Night came on and the rockets glared red in the sky. *Surely Fort McHenry can't hold out much longer*, Key thought. *When morning comes, they'll be waving a flag of surrender.*

"Oh, God, please help them," he prayed. "If it by your will, let America remain free. If our cause is just, preserve us by Your great power." He continued to pace the deck and pray until the sun shed its first rays of light.

Then Key looked west toward Fort McHenry. "The stars and stripes are still waving!" he shouted with joy. In spite of the fierce attack, the American army had held its position. Baltimore was safe!

Key reached into his pocket for a pencil and paper. He often expressed his strongest feelings by writing poems, and this was certainly one of the most exciting moments in his life.

He quickly scribbled the words that came into his mind.

Oh, say, can you see, by the dawn's early light,
What so proudly we hailed at the twilight's last gleaming?

When he finished making notes for his poem, Key stuffed the paper in his pocket and boarded the American ship. They were free to return to Baltimore.

How good it feels to be back in the land of the free and the home of the brave! Key thought. He thanked God for answering his prayers. Then he finished writing his poem.

The phrase "In God We Trust" is our national motto. It comes from the fourth stanza of "The Star Spangled Banner," where Key wrote, "This be our motto, in God is Our Trust." By law, this motto is placed on our money and engraved on the walls of both the House and Senate Chambers.

Everyone wanted to hear about Key's adventure. So he told his story and read his poem. His brother-in-law had it printed and passed out to the people of Baltimore. A musician noticed the words could be sung to a popular tune, and soon the whole city was singing it.

After peace came to the United States, Francis Key became a district attorney in Washington, D.C. He also taught Sunday School and wrote poems, many of them about his faith in God.

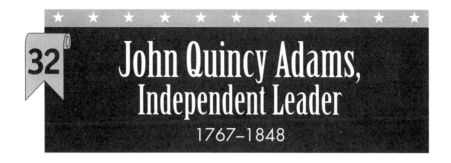

John Quincy Adams, Independent Leader
1767–1848

32

Ambassador John Adams stood beside his eleven-year-old son. The two looked out from the ship's deck across the vast Atlantic Ocean. "It's great to have you with me on this trip to France, Johnny," Adams said. "I know you're a big help to your mother when I'm away from home, and she will miss you. But I think this time in Europe will give you an excellent education."

The boy nodded. His usually serious face burst into a quick smile. "Thank you for letting me come along," he said. Then serious again and standing as tall as his short height would let him, he added, "I won't disappoint you, Father."

"I'm sure you won't, Mr. Johnny," his father said, matching his son's solemn face and tone of voice. Inside, he felt a warm glow of pride.

For the next three years, Johnny Adams went wherever his father's diplomatic assignments took him. He attended school in France, the Netherlands, and Russia. As they traveled, he quickly learned the languages of each country. Everyone was amazed at his intelligence and grown-up manners.

One day Francis Dana, the new U.S. ambassador to Russia said, "Adams, I'd like to have your son as my translator. His Russian and English are perfect, and his years with you have made him something of an expert in diplomatic matters."

John Quincy Adams was only fourteen, but his father and the U.S. government agreed he would make a fine translator. He served in Russia

until 1783 when his father asked him to come to Paris. "I need you as my secretary during the peace treaty meetings," Adams wrote his son. "You will get to see first hand the end of our long war for American independence."

After seven years in Europe and Great Britain, John decided it was time to go home. He told his father, "I don't want to be away from America so long that I become a stranger to its ways."

His father nodded in agreement. "Then I suppose it is time for you to enroll in Harvard. Although, I doubt it will take you long to learn all they can teach you."

Sure enough, John Quincy Adams graduated from college in just two years. Then he became a lawyer, but he found he didn't enjoy routine court cases. Next he wrote some excellent essays about politics and government for the newspaper. The people of Massachusetts were impressed and sent him to Congress as their senator. But when he voted as he believed rather than as they told him to vote, they were very angry and eager to get rid of him.

For the next six years, Adams served his country as an ambassador. Then in 1817 when James Monroe became President, he asked John Quincy Adams to be his Secretary of State. In this important job, Adams took charge of the United States' business with countries around the world.

Monroe and Adams soon became the best of friends. They agreed that America should make its own decisions about dealing with other governments, rather than following England's example. They also believed the U.S. needed more room to grow. They worked hard on a plan to stop other countries from claiming any land in America.

> John Quincy Adams said, "The Bible is, of all books in the world, the one which does the most to make us good, wise, and happy. The earlier my children begin to read it regularly, the more sure I am they will grow up to be useful citizens of their country and a real blessing to their parents." Perhaps you would like to take his advice of reading something from the Bible each day. How about starting with Adams' favorite part, found in Matthew 5:1–16.

In 1823, President Monroe told Adams it was time to speak up for their ideas. Since Adams agreed and wasn't afraid of taking a stand for what he believed in, he told the Russian ambassador, "The American continents are no longer open for any new European colonies." Of course, this didn't make other countries happy, but they realized the U.S. was becoming strong enough to back up what it said.

While Adams served as Secretary of State, he helped the United States claim more territory. Great Britain agreed to share its claim on the Oregon country with the U.S. Spain agreed to sell Florida. And Russia was stopped in its move toward the Pacific Northwest.

In 1825, John Quincy Adams began his four years as President. He was the first American president inaugurated in the U.S. Capitol, a new building that wasn't completely finished at that time. Adams had some great plans for America—a national university, new roads and canals, and weather stations. He wanted to lead Congress in improving life for ordinary people. But he had powerful enemies who thought he shouldn't be president. They did everything they could to ruin his plans, and they almost succeeded.

After his unhappy time in the White House, people expected Adams to go back to his home in Quincy, Massachusetts, and retire from public service. He surprised them by agreeing to represent his state in Congress. For the next seventeen years, he was a member of the U.S. House of Representatives. The other Congressmen gave him two nicknames—"Old Man Eloquent," because he was an excellent public speaker, and "Hell-Hound of Slavery," because he never let up in his fight against what he thought was an evil practice.

As more and more people spoke out against slavery, Congress got tired of hearing their requests for change. The representatives of the slave-holding states demanded that these requests be silenced. Congress agreed, but John Quincy Adams didn't. Year after year, he fought the gag rule that forbade anyone to talk about ending slavery. He never hesitated to tell people, "Slavery is the great filthy stain on the North American Union."

When Adams presented petitions [requests] from citizens, including slaves, the Southern representatives shouted, "Throw him out! He's breaking all the rules." But Adams stood firm. "No, you are breaking the rules," he said to them. "Our Constitution gives every person in the country the right to free speech." At the end of 1844, he won his battle. That night he wrote in his diary, "Blessed, forever blessed, be the name of God!"

Throughout his long life of public service, John Quincy Adams turned to the Bible and church services for encouragement. He started each day by reading several chapters in the Bible and thinking about their meaning for his life. In this way, he read through the entire Bible every year.

Although Adams' strong opinions and independent ways kept him from being as popular as other politicians, he had no regrets. "May I never stop being grateful for the many blessings God has given me," he wrote in his diary not long before he died. "And may I never be unhappy over what He has not given me. I ask His forgiveness for all the mistakes of my life."

Aloha!" the island people called to the sailors from the New England whale-hunting ship. "Come back soon!" they said, broad smiles on their pleasant faces.

As the men climbed into a small boat that would take them back to their ship, a young voice shouted, "Wait! Wait! I want to go with you!" The sailors laughed as Obookiah ran toward them. "Please take me with you to the land of books and schools," he begged.

The men shook their heads. "Obookiah, you are better off here where the weather is always warm and life is easy."

But Obookiah was determined. He climbed into the boat with them.

"All right, you can go with us," the captain said. "But you will have to work or we'll throw you overboard!" Then he laughed.

Obookiah's face lit up with joy. He reached for an oar and started rowing the boat out to sea.

Many months went by before the ship reached New England. During those months, Obookiah learned more English and dreamed about reading and writing.

When the ship sailed into Long Island Sound, Obookiah looked eagerly toward the shore. "Where can I go to learn?" he asked one of the sailors.

With a playful twinkle in his eyes, the man said, "We'll be landing at New Haven soon. It is the home of a great school called Yale. Maybe they'll know what to do with you."

As soon as he reached land, Obookiah asked the sailors to show him where to find Yale. By the time he found the college, night had come. Tired from his travels, Obookiah fell asleep outside the great building.

The next morning when the students awoke and started their busy day, they found the young Hawaiian on their steps. "Please, I want to learn," he told them, tears in his eyes.

Of course, Obookiah couldn't attend college classes. But one of the students decided to help him learn to read. He also taught him from the Bible about God's love and forgiveness of wrongdoing.

Obookiah learned quickly and soon became a Christian. "Perhaps God will use you to go back and teach your people about Jesus Christ," his tutor said.

"Yes, I would like that very much," said Obookiah. He continued to study with that goal in mind. But his body didn't like the cold New England winters. He became sick and died.

His American friends were very sad. "Now who will take God's Word to the island people?" one of the ministers asked.

If your family takes a vacation trip to Hawaii, be sure to see the Mission Houses and Kawaiahao Church, the oldest church in Honolulu. It is here King Kamehameha III is thought to have said, "The life of the land is perpetuated in righteousness"—or, as we might say, "Christian character makes a land strong." His words are Hawaii's state motto and are found at the bottom of the state seal. To understand where he got this idea, look up Proverbs 14:34 in a modern translation of the Bible.

Many young men and women quickly volunteered. About a year after Obookiah's death, the first American missionaries—fourteen in all—sailed from Boston to Hawaii. Before their ship began its long journey, they received final directions from the head of their mission group. "You are to open your hearts wide and set your goals high," he told them. "Aim at covering the islands with fields, houses, schools, and churches."

During the five-month trip, a young Yale graduate named Hiram Bingham became leader of the missionary team. "Our first job will be learning the language," he told the others.

"Yes, and then while you men build the churches and translate the

Bible," his wife Sybil said, "I and the other women can start schools and teach."

When the missionaries arrived, they learned that many changes had happened since Obookiah left Hawaii. The year before the Americans arrived, King Kamehameha II and his mother, Queen Ka'ahumanu, had commanded their people to stop making human sacrifices and worshiping idols. They also stopped the old taboos [rules] that forbade nobles and common people to talk or eat with each other. All these changes made it much easier for the American missionaries to teach the Hawaiians new ways.

When Sybil Bingham started her school, the queen attended it. In 1823, she decided to become a Christian. Several female chiefs attending the school also turned from the old gods to faith in Jesus Christ.

After her baptism, the chieftain Kapiolani said, "I am no longer afraid of Pele (the goddess thought to live in the heart of Hawaii's volcanoes). "I want to show my people how foolish they are to believe in Pele, and I think I know how," she said.

One day, Kapiolani told all her family and friends, "Follow me." Then she climbed up the side of a mountain covered with lava. When she reached the top, she looked into the crater and threw rocks and angry words down where Pele was supposed to live.

Those watching expected Pele to reach out and pull Kapiolani into the hot lava. But nothing happened.

When Kapiolani came back down the mountain, she said, "See, there is no Pele! There is only Jehovah, the true God, and He is the one we should worship." Because of Kapiolani's faith, many more Hawaiians became Christians.

Before Queen Ka'ahumanu died in 1832, the missionaries finished the first Hawaiian New Testament. She told everyone how good it was. Seven years later, the entire Bible could be read in the native language.

By 1841, over sixty missionaries lived in Hawaii and a sixth of its people had become Christians. Along with their teaching about the Christian faith, missionaries like Hiram and Sybil Bingham also brought American ways of thinking and living. And that is how far-off Hawaii came to be part of the United States.

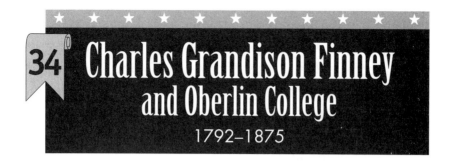

Charles Grandison Finney
and Oberlin College
1792–1875

It's interesting how many times our law books point back to the ancient laws of Moses," Finney said to his law teacher, attorney Benjamin Wright. "I've attended church all my life, but I think I'll have to make a serious study of the Bible to understand what it's all about."

"That's a good idea, Charles," the lawyer said. "It certainly can't do you any harm."

Finney immediately began to read the Old Testament story of how Moses received the laws of God and gave them to the people. He became so interested, he kept reading through the Bible. He asked his pastor George Gale to help him understand some of the more difficult parts, but mostly he just turned the ideas over and over in his mind.

As Finney read the Bible, he realized it wasn't just an interesting book filled with stories and laws. It was a book that asked him to make a decision about his relationship with God.

One beautiful fall morning in 1821, he took a walk in the woods. As he walked, he thought, *Today is the day. I will give my heart to God before I come out of these woods*. He knelt beside a fallen log and began to pray. Immediately, he felt peace and love flow into his heart.

The next morning, Finney went to work as usual. But when he met with a man who wanted his legal advice, he delivered his surprising news. "I'm sorry, sir," Finney told the man, "I won't be able to help you. I have been asked by the Lord Jesus Christ to present His case." Finney said goodbye to the law office and began to study so he could become a preacher.

When he was thirty-one, Finney started preaching in the churches of upper New York state. Some people liked his interesting style of speaking and the way he made the Bible easy to understand. Others thought he pushed people too hard to act on what the Bible said. "He talks like a lawyer arguing a case in front of a jury," most of the ministers said. "It isn't proper."

About two years after Finney started preaching, larger crowds began to come to his meetings. "You don't need to wait for something miraculous to happen to you," Finney told them. "You can become a Christian right now just by deciding to turn from your old ways to follow Jesus Christ." Hundreds took his challenge. Soon Finney received invitations to preach in the big cities of New York, Philadelphia, and Boston.

Finney's greatest success as an evangelist came in Rochester, New York. Store owners shut their doors and encouraged everyone in town to go hear Finney. Doctors, lawyers, businessmen, and teachers attended the services. Many of them repented of their selfish ways and started looking for ways to help the needy. People began to call Finney's revival the Second Great Awakening.

For several years, Finney traveled all the time. But his body became tired and sick, so he settled down to pastor in New York City. Thousands of New Yorkers regularly came to hear him preach. As a pastor, he took a stand against allowing slave owners to receive Communion. He also spoke out against charging rent for pews. Most churches expected people to pay a yearly fee, a kind of rent for their space in the church. Finney pointed out how unfair this was to the poor. In the Broadway Tabernacle where he pastored, the poor were welcome to take the best seats in the house.

Many of Finney's followers decided to train for Christian service. They were unhappy when the schools they attended disagreed with Finney's teaching, especially his teaching against slavery. So they made a deal with a new college in Oberlin, Ohio. "If you'll invite Charles Finney to come and teach here, and if you'll allow black students here too, we'll all enroll in your school." The college officials agreed.

In 1835, Finney started teaching at Oberlin. He also pastored a large church there—the largest west of the Allegheny Mountains. In a few years, he became the college's president. Every summer, he traveled in the East to hold revival meetings. Twice he traveled to England, and crowds there flocked to hear him. He even had a part in encouraging some British Christians to start the YMCA (Young Men's Christian Association) and the Salvation Army.

Everywhere he went, Finney taught people that God wanted them to make a difference in the world. "The Christian's main job is reforming individual lives, communities, and governments," he told them. "We must show compassion for those in slavery, for those whose lives are destroyed by drinking, for people out on the streets, and for all the miserable of the earth."

The students of Oberlin took him seriously. Soon their college was considered the center of the growing movement to end slavery. When the Underground Railroad (a chain of rescue stations leading from the South into Canada) began taking slaves to freedom, Oberlin became a main stop on six different escape routes.

You can visit Oberlin College, the school Finney loved so much, in Oberlin, Ohio. Its library has a collection of photographs of Finney, along with interesting magazines and books by and about him. Another great place to find out more about Finney is the Billy Graham Center at Wheaton College in Wheaton, Illinois. It specializes in presenting the history of evangelism, revivals, and missions.

Oberlin professors and students also wanted to end prejudice in the North. The college took pride in offering black people a good education at a low cost and treating them with the same respect given to white students.

At the time Charles Finney came to Oberlin, most colleges allowed only white men to earn degrees. Oberlin welcomed women students, and in 1841 graduated the first three American women to ever receive bachelor's degrees.

Because of Finney's teaching, Christians became excited about sharing their faith with others. They also got busy helping those in need. Finney helped organize many of their volunteer groups into what he called the *Benevolent Empire* (we might call it a *Generous Kingdom*). Together, these groups spent almost as much money helping people in a year as the U.S. government spent on its entire operation. And it came from caring, unselfish people, not from taxes.

Throughout his long ministry, Charles Finney called people to follow God's ways. He didn't think there should be a difference between what people said in church and what they did at work, at home, in their schools, or in running their nation. "God cannot support this free and blessed country," Finney said, "unless Christians take a stand for what is right. They must vote for honest leaders and do their duty to their country as a part of their duty to God."

Because of Finney's teaching and his followers' actions, America became a better place to live.

A mericans don't know how to spell!" Noah Webster, the young school teacher-lawyer said in an annoyed voice. "Children and grownups put down words however they please. They write *jinerll* instead of *general*, *toune* instead of *town*, or *contery* instead of *country*."

Perhaps there's some way I can help them, Webster thought. He decided that Americans needed more simple rules of spelling than the British used. Besides, spelling things differently in America would encourage the printing of more American books. He also thought it would bind Americans together to have their own special language.

"Let us spell and speak in our own way," he said, "instead of blindly following the British." To help Americans learn to spell alike, he created what everyone called Webster's Blue-Backed Speller. In this textbook, he included rules for good behavior from the Bible.

It was a huge success, and soon Webster began dreaming of a much larger book—a complete dictionary of the American language. But other important responsibilities kept him busy much of the time.

In 1803, he moved to New Haven, Connecticut, and spent all his time creating a dictionary. Three years later, his *Compendious Dictionary of the English Language* was finished. Although it listed 5,000 words no other English dictionary contained, Webster wasn't satisfied. He had in mind a much larger dictionary. But he also became interested in the history of epidemics, weather, agriculture, economics, and banking. One idea led to another, and they all turned into books.

Then one day in 1825, he received a letter from his publisher. "Mr. Webster, we are happy to tell you, your Elementary Spelling Book has sold fifteen million copies since we published it in 1783." Noah shook his head in amazement. "That's a lot of Blue-Backed Spellers," he said to himself. Then he continued reading the letter, "As you probably know, your grammar and reading books are also among the most popular textbooks in America. Congratulations on making a great contribution to education."

"If you think that's something," Webster said, "wait until you see my new dictionary!"

"What did you say, Noah?" his wife asked.

But Noah didn't hear her. The word-lover was already back at work on his enormous project.

After twenty-six years of studying words, Webster had decided to quit doing anything besides putting together his dictionary. The book kept growing larger and larger— Native American words, frontier words, Bible words, scientific and technical words.

When he finished, Webster called his wife into his office, "Let us give thanks to God," he said. "The work is complete." The two prayed to the One they firmly believed had given people the gift of words.

★ ★ ★ ★ ★ ★

You can visit the house where Noah Webster wrote his dictionary. It is part of Henry Ford's Greenfield Village Museum in Dearborn, Michigan. In a 260-acre park, Ford brought the homes, offices, and laboratories of many great inventors. Some of them, like the home of Webster, had to be moved across several states. If Noah Webster could welcome you to his home, he would tell you what he once told America: "Education is useless without the Bible."

In the introduction to his dictionary, Webster wrote, "In my opinion, the Christian religion is the most important and one of the first things in which all children should be instructed. It is clear to me, any government that intends to protect the rights of free people must be based on Christianity."

Noah Webster's dictionary held 12,000 more words and 40,000 more definitions than any other dictionary of the English language. Within twenty years of its first printing, 24,000,000 copies of Webster's dictionary had been purchased by Americans.

36 Samuel Finley Breese Morse, Father of the Telegraph
1791–1872

Morse half listened as those seated around the dinner table talked. He didn't know anyone on board the ship *Sully,* but he supposed that would change during the voyage from Europe to America. *If only there were some way to get there quicker*, he thought. After three years of intense art study, he was sure he could paint grand historical scenes for the U.S. Capitol Building. He could hardly wait to get started.

While he daydreamed about painting, the table talk turned to science and new inventions. Something he heard caught Morse's attention. "I'm sorry," he said to the man across the table. "I missed what you just said about electricity."

"Oh, I was just saying that scientists have learned it's possible for electricity to travel instantly down a length of wire," the man repeated. "I saw it done and it's fascinating, although what good it is to anyone I don't know."

Morse drifted back into his own thoughts. *If electricity can travel down a wire, I wonder if it could somehow be used to send messages.* He turned the idea around and around in his mind. Remembering the electrical experiments his math and science teachers at Yale had presented, he thought about how he could test his idea.

After dinner, he went back to his cabin and began to draw some simple machines for controlling the flow of electricity. The more he thought about it, the more excited he became. During the rest of the trip home, all he could think about was his new project.

By the time he reached New York Harbor, Morse knew how he would build his new machine. He had a name for it, too—the telegraph. Just before he left the ship, he told its captain, "Well, captain, if you hear of the telegraph one of these days, remember the discovery was made on the good ship *Sully*."

Then he waved to his brothers, Richard and Sidney, and hurried to greet them. Since he had spent all he had on art lessons, he accepted their offer of a room on top of their newspaper building. "But it's just for a little while," he said. "Then I'll be going to Washington, D.C., to paint."

Unfortunately, Morse's dream didn't come true. The assignment of painting the Capitol's domed ceiling went to another artist. To support himself, he began to teach painting and sculpture at New York University.

The rest of his time went to building his telegraph and working out a code to use in sending messages on it. He continued to live in the one dreary room his brothers provided, cooking all his own meals—when he remembered to eat!

After five years of work, he told his fellow teacher and helper Leonard Gale, "It's time to show the world what we've got." They prepared a demonstration and invited several important men. "Very interesting!" they said. "Yes, remarkable!" But no one wanted to give Morse the money to finish his project.

One of Morse's students, Alfred Vail, attended the demonstration. "Mr. Morse, that's wonderful!" he said. "My father owns an iron and brass factory, and I'm sure I can get supplies from him to help you build a better model."

"Then you can be my business partner, Alfred," Morse said. "I'll give you a fourth of whatever we make from the telegraph."

★ ★ ★ ★ ★ ★

If you would like to see the place where Morse showed his telegraph machine in 1842, visit Castle Clinton National Monument on Manhattan Island, New York. At that time it was called Castle Garden and the people of the city went there for music concerts, fireworks, and scientific demonstrations. The year before Samuel Morse died, the telegraph operators of America honored him with a statue in New York City's Central Park.

Vail kept his word about helping. The next year, Morse took the new and improved machine to Congress. He hoped the politicians would give him money to build an electric line long enough to test it, but they said no.

For the next five years, Morse tried to find a sponsor in Europe, England, and the United States. He became weary and discouraged, but he didn't give up.

Finally, in 1843, Congress agreed to vote on whether to pay $30,000 for his experiment. He paced the halls, waiting for the vote. In a letter to his wife, he wrote, "The only gleam of hope is from confidence in God. When I look upward it calms my fears for the future, and I seem to hear a voice saying, 'If I clothe the lilies of the field, shall I not also clothe you?' This is my strong confidence, and I will wait patiently for God's direction."

Many great art collections proudly display Morse's paintings. His painting of the House of Representatives hangs in Statuary Hall in Washington, D.C. He is considered one of the best American artists of his time.

As evening came, Morse decided the vote wouldn't take place. He went to his hotel room and packed. For a while he felt worried and sad. Then he remembered that God was watching over him and he went to sleep.

The next morning, a friend brought Morse a message. "Congratulations!" the young woman said. "Your bill passed!"

"Annie, are you sure?" Morse asked.

"Positive."

With a broad smile and tears in his eyes, Morse said, "Thank you for bringing me this wonderful news. Since you were the first to tell me, you will also be the first to receive a message over my telegraph."

A year later, Morse sent a message to Annie along the line that had been strung between Baltimore and Washington. He tapped out a series of dots and dashes that stood for letters of the alphabet. Then he and those with him in Baltimore waited for Annie to repeat the message back correctly.

Her dots and dashes sent it back perfectly. The message read, ["What wonders God has done!"] (He actually quoted Numbers 23:23 from the

King James Version of the Bible which reads, "What hath God wrought!").
Samuel Morse had chosen these words from the Bible to honor the One he
believed had made his success possible.

In the years that followed, wealth and world-wide fame came to the
inventor of the telegraph. He went on inventing, giving America its first
camera called a daguerreotype, and he also experimented with underwater
telegraph lines. He looked ahead with hope and joy, but not because of
his accomplishments. "The nearer I come to the end of my life," he told a
friend, "the clearer the truth of the Bible is to me and the more I appre-
ciate His salvation. Because of Him, the future is bright!"

37 Missionaries on the Oregon Trial
1836–1874

Marcus and Narcissa Prentiss Whitman
Henry and Eliza Spaulding

Narcissa Whitman gripped the wagon seat as her husband Marcus urged their team of oxen to pull harder. "Oh, God, keep us out of the quicksand," she quietly prayed.

"Everyone says this river crossing is the worst part of the journey to Oregon Territory," Marcus told her.

She smiled to let him know she was all right. "If God wants us to take His Word to the Cayuse Indians, I'm sure He'll get us there safely. Besides I have my very own doctor to look after me." The wagon lurched forward and Narcissa said another prayer, this time for missionaries Eliza and Henry Spaulding in the wagon behind them.

Day after day, the covered wagons of settlers and fur traders rolled west. All along the way, Narcissa exclaimed with delight, "What beautiful country!" or "Look at that! Isn't God's creation amazing?"

Not all the travelers' experiences were enjoyable. Sometimes people on the trial got hurt or sick. Often the pioneers had to leave behind things they really needed so their weary teams and broken wagons could keep moving. At night Narcissa wrote about her new experiences in her journal.

In September 1836, after traveling for five months, the Whitmans and the Spauldings reached their goal—Fort Walla Walla, where the Columbia and Walla Walla rivers met. From here they would separate and start their missions.

Marcus and Narcissa settled among the Cayuse tribe at Waiilatpu in the beautiful green valley of the Walla Walla River. The Spauldings went a little further north, above the Snake River, to Lapwai and the Nez Percé tribe. They didn't have a lovely place to live like the Whitmans, but the Nez Percé were eager to have them come.

The missionaries' first job was getting ready for winter. They built rough little shelters and made sure they had enough food stored up. They also began their study of the Native American languages. In the evenings the Cayuse men and boys liked to come to the Whitmans' home and learn to sing hymns.

During the next six years, the Whitmans created a large farm and mission center. It had its own gristmill and blacksmith shop. Besides the everyday work of running a large farm and home on the frontier, Marcus and Narcissa learned the Cayuse language, took care of the sick, taught Cayuse and white children, and welcomed the growing number of pioneers who came to the area.

★ ★ ★ ★ ★ ★

You can learn more about early settlement in the Oregon country (including Oregon, Washington, Idaho, western Wyoming, and Montana) by visiting the Whitman Mission National Historic Site in Walla Walla, Washington. The museum and library have an interesting collection of items from the Whitman Mission and the Cayuse Indians. You'll also see photos showing how archaeologists went about digging up history at the mission. In nearby Spaulding, Idaho, you can visit the Nez Percé National Historical Park, site of the Spaulding mission.

In 1842 Marcus traveled back east to do business with the directors of his mission. He also asked President Tyler not to let the Oregon country be taken over by any other nation. Before he returned, a large group of American settlers asked Marcus to be their trail guide and doctor from Independence, Missouri, to Oregon. When the wagon train started west, it held 1,000 people. Over one hundred of them died on the journey, but the rest settled in the Willamette River valley. They were soon joined by thousands more who heard about the rich land of the Oregon territory.

As white settlement increased and the Whitman mission grew, the

Cayuse disliked the white people more and more. "It is your fault all these strangers are coming to take our land," they told Marcus. "We don't want your God and we don't want to be farmers." But the Whitmans kept hoping things would change. In the meantime, they offered help to more and more American settlers and adopted seven children whose parents had died on the Oregon trail. Often over seventy people lived at the mission station.

Then, in 1847, measles and smallpox came west with the settlers. The Cayuse began to die from the white man's sickness. "Let me help you," Marcus Whitman begged them. "I am a doctor and I have medicines." He did his best, but in two months, half of the tribe died.

The Cayuse didn't understand what was happening. "It is that white man's fault," they told each other. "He is poisoning our people with his medicine."

Five angry men of the tribe decided to make the missionaries pay for the trouble they had brought. They got their tomahawks, covered them with blankets, and went to the Whitmans' home. When they saw Marcus Whitman sitting beside the fire reading, one of the braves rushed up behind him and struck him on the head. Narcissa heard the noise and came to see what was happening.

★ ★ ★ ★ ★ ★

When you visit the nation's Capitol building in Washington, D.C., you will see the statue of Dr. Marcus Whitman in Statuary Hall. He is depicted in action, wearing his buckskin suit, a coonskin cap, and carrying his medical bag and books to his next missionary task.

"No!" she screamed when she saw Marcus on the floor. The Cayuse turned and killed her. Within minutes, Narcissa and Marcus lay dead, along with twelve white men visiting the mission. Around sixty women and children in the mission were held prisoners for five weeks.

When American troops came to the rescue, they also told other missionaries in the area to leave. "But the Nez Percé want us here," Henry Spaulding told them. "It isn't the same for us as the Whitmans."

"It's just too dangerous, Reverend Spaulding," the commander said.

So Henry and Eliza packed up and said good-bye to their Native American friends. "We will see you again, either here or in heaven," they promised.

After the Whitman massacre, American settlers in the Oregon country begged the U.S. government to make it a territory and protect it. The U.S. agreed and began giving large pieces of free land to Americans who were willing to settle there.

In 1871, Henry Spaulding returned to the Nez Percé. Hundreds of them became Christians and took their new religious faith to other tribes in the Pacific Northwest.

Daniel Webster,
Defender of the Union
1782–1852

During a break from congressional business, the southern senators gathered around South Carolina's senator Robert Hayne. They spoke in low voices, but their faces and gestures made it clear they were excited.

"They're hatching up some plan over there," Senator Daniel Webster of Massachusetts said to the senators seated near him.

"Oh, it's just Hayne again," said one of them. "He's telling them how the states have a right to ignore any national law they disagree with. And, of course, they all agree."

Webster nodded. "They've been mad about the tariff laws for years, and it's not getting better." (By tariff, he meant the special tax on things purchased from foreign countries.)

> Webster believed the Bible was good for our country and that "whatever makes people good Christians also makes them good Americans."

"Well, it isn't right for them to buy from England and France when we make the same things right here in America," another Northern senator said. "Even though President Jackson supports the tariff, Vice President Calhoun is on the side of the South. He's encouraging Hayne to keep up the fight here in the Senate."

"Congress is now in session!" a voice boomed out, calling the senators back to their seats. Senator Hayne asked to speak and the room became silent. He made a long, carefully planned speech about the rights of individual states. Then he accused the northeastern states of passing laws that benefited their industries and hurt the rest of the country.

When Hayne finished, Senator Webster stood to speak. Point by point, he argued against what Hayne had said. "Massachusetts doesn't need me to defend it against Senator Hayne's charges," he said. "There is Boston and Concord and Lexington and Bunker Hill." Everyone knew he was reminding them of how much Massachusetts had done to help create the United States.

Webster sat down and Hayne stood to speak again. With harsh words, he attacked New England, former President Madison's war with England, and Daniel Webster. Then he sat down as the Southern and some of the Western senators clapped in approval.

Webster stood calmly and looked around the room at his fellow senators. He began to speak as though talking to them over dinner. He went on talking and talking and talking for two days. The longer he talked, the more fiery his speech became. The senators sat quietly, giving him their full attention.

As he reached the end of his magnificent speech, Webster said, "When I see the sun for the last time, I hope it will not be shining on the broken pieces of a once great Union; on states separated, quarreling, warlike; on a land torn apart with feuds, or covered with the blood of its fathers, sons, and brothers."

Many historians think that Daniel Webster was one of the greatest speakers who ever lived. He explained his talent in this way: "If there is anything in my thoughts or style to praise, the credit is due to my parents for teaching me to love the Scriptures when I was young."

Pointing to the United States flag, he continued, "Now known and respected throughout the earth . . . Not a stripe erased or a single star removed . . . It does not stand for 'Liberty first and Union afterwards,' but rather 'Liberty and Union, now and forever, one and unbroken!'"

Many of the senators stood and cheered. Some of them brushed tears from their eyes. A few of those who had opposed him wondered if perhaps he was right. Everyone knew it was the greatest speech Webster had ever given.

In the years that followed, a feeling of division continued to grow between the Southern and Northern states. The South wanted new U.S. states and territories to accept slavery. The North didn't. The South wanted free trade with foreign countries. The North didn't. In many ways, the country seemed to be splitting in two, and each side tried to hold on to the West.

In 1850, Henry Clay worked out a compromise agreement between the North and the South. In this deal, each side would get part of what they wanted. Most of the Northern senators thought it was wrong because it allowed slavery to continue. But Daniel Webster encouraged them to go along with it. "I wish to speak today," he told his fellow senators, "not as a Massachusetts man, nor as a Northern man, but as an American . . . I speak today for the preservation [safekeeping] of the Union."

★ ★ ★ ★ ★ ★

"If we stay true to the teaching of the Bible, our country will go on prospering. But if we and future generations neglect its instructions and authority, no one can tell what sudden disaster may crush us and bury all our glory in darkness."

Daniel Webster

For the next three hours, he argued that the new territories and states should be allowed to decide about slavery for themselves. He knew that most of them would not allow slaves. At the end of his speech he said, "I would rather hear of war, disease, and famine than to hear gentlemen talk about secession . . . No, Sir! No, Sir! There can be no secession!"

The compromise passed, and the United States held together . . . at least for a while. And for many years to come, especially during the nation's Civil War, people quoted Daniel Webster's last great speech.

39 Elijah Parish Lovejoy, Newspaper Man with a Mission
1802–1837

I don't have all day for you to think about pulling this plow," Elijah said to the horse. "Father will expect us to be through plowing this field by the time he finishes writing his Sunday sermon."

As if he understood, the horse moved forward. Elijah said, "Good boy!" and started to sing one of his favorite hymns. The work always seemed to go faster when he sang or recited the hundreds of Bible verses he knew by heart.

As the oldest of nine children on a farm in Maine, Elijah was used to plenty of hard work. But it wasn't all with his muscles. He liked stretching his mind and making it work too. He'd learned to read at the age of four, and his teachers at the village school said he had a talent for writing.

When Elijah attended college, he discovered more about his gift with words. He wrote poetry and essays that won him many compliments. And when he graduated with his school's highest honors, everyone said, "That young man is sure to be a success!"

After graduation, Elijah started a private high school in St. Louis. In his extra time, he wrote a few poems and articles for the *St. Louis Times*. Gradually, he realized that he wanted to write more than anything else. So he quit teaching and went to work as a newspaper editor. It seemed he had found his calling in life. Then, about two years later, something happened that turned him in a new direction.

A preacher named David Nelson came to St. Louis. Elijah heard him talk about how God's heart was broken over people's wrongdoing, especially slavery. "It is a sin against God, who is the rightful owner of all human beings. And it

is a sin against the slaves, who should be free to answer to God."

Elijah had never owned a slave, but as Nelson preached he thought about other wrongs he had done. *I certainly haven't acted as though God owned me,* he thought. *I've done pretty much what I wanted to.*

"God, please forgive me," he prayed. "I want to spend my life serving You."

Elijah believed God wanted him to become a minister like David Nelson, so he went to Princeton University to study for the ministry. In the spring of 1833, the Presbyterian church approved him as a preacher. After preaching for a few months, Elijah realized there was more than one way of spreading God's Word. *Perhaps I can preach best through my writing!* he thought.

★ ★ ★ ★ ★ ★

While in St. Louis, Elijah Lovejoy took charge of a Presbyterian newspaper called *The St. Louis Observer*. In its pages, he spoke out against things he believed were evil, including slavery.

Some of his St. Louis friends invited Elijah to take charge of their Presbyterian newspaper called *The St. Louis Observer*. In its pages, he spoke out against things he believed were evil, including slavery.

Soon angry people gathered outside the newspaper office. "You have no right to tell us we're evil!" one man shouted. "You're nothing but a trouble maker!" another yelled. "Take your Yankee ideas and go home!" a woman screamed. Then a rock came crashing through the window of the office.

Elijah tried to talk to the people, but they refused to listen. "Missouri is a slave state, and if you don't like it, you better leave," they told him.

Day after day, the threats continued. "It isn't safe for you to stay here, Elijah," warned his friends.

"But I can't quit speaking out against what I know is wrong," he said.

"Maybe you should think about going to Illinois," one friend said. "It doesn't allow slavery, so folks shouldn't get as upset with you there."

"That's a good idea," Elijah said. He moved to Alton, just across the river from St. Louis. And he started printing his newspaper again right away.

He soon found out people in Alton believed as much in slavery as those in St. Louis. In spite of Illinois law, the town was split over what was right.

Some of Alton's rougher men decided to put a stop to Elijah's newspaper.

They got together and broke into his office at night. "Smash that printing press," their leader said. "That ought to shut him up."

But it didn't. Elijah had many friends who hated slavery, and they helped him buy another printing press. The town bullies destroyed it. Elijah ordered another printing press and went on writing. After the third press was destroyed, he asked the town to call a meeting.

When everyone had gathered, Elijah asked the man in charge of the meeting if he could speak. "Go ahead, Mr. Lovejoy," he said in a grouchy voice.

"Mr. Chairman, I want my fellow citizens to think well of me. But I will answer to God for what I've done, so I must speak up for what is right."

He looked around the meeting room at some who wished he was dead and others who took his side. "I don't expect everyone to agree with me," he said. "I ask only to be protected in my rights." Elijah turned to face the crowd and said, "I haven't committed any crime or broken any law. So why do you threaten to tar and feather me? Why do you allow mobs to destroy my property and threaten to kill me?"

Several people began to cry as Lovejoy talked about how he had been mistreated. But the town council still refused to give him any protection.

> ★ ★ ★ ★ ★ ★
>
> Twenty-one years after Elijah Lovejoy died in Alton, Abraham Lincoln visited the town to speak against slavery. In 1863, as President of the United States, Lincoln made slavery against the law in the entire United States.

"I am convinced that if I am not safe in Alton, I won't be safe any-where," Elijah said. "So after praying and talking with my friends, I've decided to stay here. I'll look to God for my safety, and if I die, I will die here."

Just four nights later, a mob broke into the warehouse where Lovejoy's fourth new printing press was stored. Hearing the noise, Elijah gathered some friends and they went with him to protect his property. Suddenly five shots rang out and Elijah Lovejoy lay dead.

After his murder on November 7, 1837, thousands of people learned about what Elijah stood for and took up his fight against slavery. Instead of putting an end to his voice, the mob had helped spread his message of freedom all across the United States.

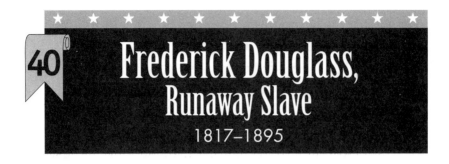

Frederick Douglass, Runaway Slave

1817–1895

F reddy, I want you to look me straight in the face when we talk," Sophia Auld kindly told the slave boy. "You're not on the plantation anymore, so don't act like a scared rabbit."

"Yes, Miss Sophia," Frederick said. He smiled at her and thought how nice it would be to live with the Aulds and take care of their little boy Tommy. The house was always pleasant because of his new mistress' singing and praying. Often she stopped in her work to look at a large book. Frederick didn't see any pictures on its pages. He wondered why she spent so much time staring at the squiggly lines inside its covers.

"Would you teach me to read?" he asked.

"Of course, I will," Mrs. Auld said. "Let's start right now."

Before long, Frederick knew the alphabet and could spell simple words. "You are a very smart boy, Freddy," Mrs. Auld told him. "Soon you'll be able to read the Bible."

Later, Mrs. Auld proudly told her husband that Frederick was turning out to be a bright student. He frowned at the black boy and then at his wife. "Sophia, you've never had slaves before, so I don't expect you to know how to treat them. But you cannot teach the boy to read."

"Why?" she exclaimed. "I thought you'd be pleased."

"It's against the law to teach slaves to read," he told her. "Learning will spoil the best slave in the world. All any slave should know is how to please his master."

Mrs. Auld did just as she was told by her husband. But from that

moment on, Frederick understood that the way out of slavery was through education. When he and little Tommy Auld played with white boys in the neighborhood, Frederick begged them to teach him how to read and write. They gave him a Webster's blue-backed speller. Then they gladly helped Frederick with his lessons. "You've got as much right to learn as anybody," one of the boys told him. "God didn't make anyone to be a slave, especially not someone as smart as you."

For the next twelve years, Frederick worked for Hugh Auld and his family in Baltimore and for Hugh's brother Thomas Auld and his family on their big plantation near Easton, Maryland. During that time, he met a black man named Charles Lawson who taught him about the Christian faith.

Frederick began to pray and felt a new love in his heart for everyone. But his hatred for slavery became even greater.

"One of these days, the Lord has a great work for you to do," Lawson told him.

"I am a slave, and a slave for life," Frederick said. "How can I do anything?"

"The Lord can set you free," Lawson said with confidence. "If you want liberty, ask the Lord for it in faith, and He will give it to you."

Sometimes Frederick would stand on the bank of the Chesapeake Bay and watch the sail boats moving out toward the ocean. He dreamed of sailing across the water into freedom. "Oh God, save me!" he prayed. "Deliver me!" Then he thought, *I cannot live and die a slave. God helping me, I will travel north and be free.*"

In the fall of 1838, Frederick's prayer was answered. With borrowed identification papers from a free black sailor and a train ticket given to him by his girlfriend, he took a train out of Baltimore and into a brand new life.

No longer was he Frederick Augustus Washington Bailey, a Southern slave. He became Frederick Douglass, a free man, and he married the young woman who had helped him escape. They settled in New Bedford, Massachusetts.

Three years after his escape, Frederick attended his first antislavery meeting. When the abolitionist leaders learned that he was an escaped slave, they asked him to speak. The crowd listened in horror as the twenty-three-year-old black man told them what it was like to grow up in slavery. They cried as he talked about how it felt to be free.

After the meeting, Frederick's hero, abolitionist William Lloyd Garrison asked him to become an agent for the American Anti-Slavery Society. For the next ten years Frederick spent most of his time traveling and speaking. He also wrote a book about his experiences, and it became one of the most popular books in America. Telling about his past took great courage because runaway slaves could be captured and taken back to their masters.

When things became too risky for Frederick and his wife, they left the country. During their long visit to England, Douglass spoke often and made many friends. These British friends collected enough money to buy his freedom from the Aulds.

When the Douglasses came back to America, they lived in Rochester, New York. Often late at night, they would welcome runaway slaves into their home. "You're safe here," Frederick told them. When they were fed and rested, he made sure they had a way to travel on to wherever they were going.

The best way to get to learn about this great man is by reading his book titled *The Life and Times of Frederick Douglass*. In its pages, he wrote, "I love the religion of our blessed Savior that comes from above and is pure, peaceable, fair, gentle, full of mercy and good deeds."

Hundreds of people in the North and South helped African Americans in this way. They called their escape routes "the underground railroad."

Frederick edited a newspaper and continued to speak out against slavery. When the Civil War began, he encouraged black men to join the army. When he heard that they were treated badly, he went to see President Lincoln and asked him to do something about it.

After the war and slavery ended, Frederick Douglass moved to Washington, D.C., As president of the Freedman's Savings and Trust Company, he helped freed slaves get a new start in life. He also served his country as U.S. Marshal for the District of Columbia and U.S. Minister to Haiti.

When Douglass learned that one of the Aulds' grown-up daughters had come to hear him speak, he went looking for her. She and her husband invited him to their home and welcomed him as a friend. "I always agreed with you about slavery," Amanda told him. "As soon as my slaves were adults, I set them all free."

Not long after that, Douglass decided to visit the Maryland plantation where he had lived as a little boy. He wanted to know what had happened to his relatives. When his former owner Captain Thomas Auld heard he was in the area, he invited him to come for a visit.

"Come sit beside my bed, Marshal Douglass," the feeble old man said.

"Not Marshal, but Frederick to you," Douglass answered. As the former master and slave shook hands, tears rolled down Auld's face. "Frederick, I always knew you were too smart to be a slave," he said. "If I had been you, I would have run away just as you did."

"You and I were both born into a way of life we didn't choose," Douglass told him. "It was wrong, but now it is past."

Every day, Isabelle and her family worked hard on their Dutch master's farm in Hurley, New York. Then at night, they huddled together in the basement of Colonel Charles Hardenbergh's house. In this damp, dark room, they tried to make a home and keep their hope alive.

"Gather 'round, children," Mama Bett said almost every evening. Isabelle knew that meant story time. She loved to hear her mother's rich voice tell about faraway times and places. Mama Bett also listened to her children's problems and did her best to comfort them.

"My children, there is a God who hears and sees you," she told them. "When you are beaten, or cruelly treated, or fall into any trouble, you must call on Him. He will always hear and help you."

When Isabelle was nine years old, Colonel Hardenbergh sold her away from her family. Her new master didn't speak Dutch like the Hardenberghs, so when Isabelle was told to do something, she did not understand the English words. For her disobedience, she was whipped across her back until blood came.

As she cried herself to sleep at night, Isabelle remembered her mother's words about asking God for help. She began to tell Him her troubles every day just as she would have talked to Mama Bett. Sometimes she felt sure she heard Him answer.

Before her thirteenth birthday, she had learned English and could understand instructions. As Belle finished growing up and started her own family, she heard how the people of New York were gradually changing their minds about slavery. The state passed a law on July 4, 1827, to set all its slaves free.

Some wonderful Quakers helped Belle get a new start in life. They told her, "You have no master now except God."

That same year, Belle had an amazing experience. While having one of her daily talks with God, she saw a bright light all around her. "Who are you?" she asked, aware that someone was with her. "It's Jesus!" she said. From that day on, she was sure the Bible stories about the Savior rising from the dead was really true.

Although she was free, Belle still had many hard times and was often mistreated. In 1829, she went to work as a housekeeper in New York City. After several years, she decided life in a big city was another kind of slavery. Wealthy people lived in mansions, while the poor and people just arriving from Europe suffered in the city's slums. "Here the rich rob the poor and the poor rob each other," she told a friend.

In 1843, Belle left the city and went east. *Lord, I need a new name for my new life*, Belle thought. In her mind, she heard Him say, "Your name is Sojourner because you are to travel up and down the land, showing people their sins." Since God was her Good Master now and His name was Truth, Sojourner took His name as her last name.

Wherever Sojourner Truth traveled, she told everyone who would listen about God. She supported herself by doing small jobs in homes. When she wasn't working or traveling, she preached, sang, and prayed in the streets. Often she visited religious and reform meetings. Many times she spoke, even when she wasn't one of the scheduled speakers. People listened

in amazement to this six-foot-tall black woman with a deep, strong voice. Although she wore a simple dress, Sojourner had the confidence and dignity of a queen. Whenever she spoke, people listened.

As she traveled from town to town, Sojourner discovered that many Americans—white and black—were working hard to end slavery. They called themselves *abolitionists* because they wanted to put an end to slavery in the entire United States. They asked her to speak in most of their gatherings.

Sojourner also found out that women in America were beginning to speak up for their rights. Since she believed God made all His children to be respected and fully free to use their abilities, she supported their cause and spoke in many of their meetings.

Just before the Civil War, Sojourner visited Iowa. As she traveled, she heard farmers talking about how insects called weevils had destroyed their wheat crop. The fields of wheat looked just fine to Sojourner. But when she looked closely at the grain, she could see that it had been eaten up from inside.

She traveled on to a religious meeting and took a seat near the front of the room. One of the speakers talked about the greatness of the U.S. Constitution and how it protected the rights of all Americans. Sojourner listened until he finished. Then she stood and began to speak.

"Children, I talk to God and He talks to me," she told the crowd. "I talk to God in the fields and woods. This morning I was walking and I saw the wheat holding up its head, looking very big. I went up and took hold of it. Would you believe it, there was no wheat there?" Everyone in the meeting knew just what she meant.

"I asked God, 'What's the matter with this wheat?'" she continued. "And He said to me, 'Sojourner, there is a little weevil in it.'"

She paused and looked at the man who had spoken just before her. "Now I hear talking about the Constitution and the rights of man. I come up and I take hold of this Constitution. It looks mighty big, and I feel for my rights, but there ain't any there."

Here and there in the crowd, people began to chuckle. Sojourner went on speaking. "Then I said, 'God, what's the matter with this Constitution?' He said to me, 'Sojourner, there is a little weevil in it.'"

Of course, slavery was the "weevil" she was talking about.

For twenty-one years, Sojourner traveled from the New England states, around the Great Lakes, across the Midwest, and into the frontier towns of Missouri and Kansas. During the Civil War, she helped raise money for black regiments.

At the age of sixty-four she decided to go to Washington, D.C. and talk to President Lincoln. He was eager to meet this brave African American who had done so much to help end slavery. He invited her to come to the White House.

Although Sojourner couldn't read or write, she kept an autograph book. In her *Book of Life*, she collected signatures of important people she met. When she handed it to President Lincoln, he wrote, "For Aunty Sojourner Truth, October 29, 1864." She was proud to call him her friend.

After the war Sojourner went to work for the National Freedmen's Relief Association, a group that helped freed slaves find homes and work.

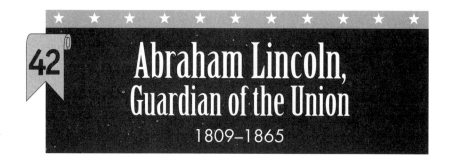

42 Abraham Lincoln, Guardian of the Union
1809–1865

Abraham Lincoln glanced out an upstairs window in his Springfield, Illinois, home. "Look at all those people out there who've come to see us off to Washington," he said to his wife. With a mischievous twinkle in his eyes, he added, "From the size of that crowd, I'd say folks are mighty eager to get rid of us."

"Abraham, that's ridiculous!" Mary Lincoln scolded. "They're just so proud of you. They all feel as if they're going to the White House with you."

"Then I better say a few words to them." Lincoln opened the window and waved. The people cheered. Deeply touched by their affection, the newly elected President talked about how hard it was to leave his home and law office and the people he loved. Then his thoughts turned to the terrible trouble that was threatening to tear the Northern and Southern states apart.

"I now leave, not knowing when or if I will return. The task before me is greater than that which rested upon Washington," Lincoln said sadly. "Without the help of that Divine Being who always helped him, I cannot succeed. With God's help I cannot fail. Trusting in Him who can go with me, and remain with you, and be everywhere for good, let us confidently hope that all will yet be well."

But all was not well in the spring of 1861. Soon after Lincoln officially became president, the Confederate Army fired on Fort Sumter. Instead of fighting an outside enemy, the United States was at war with itself. During the first year of the war, President Lincoln grew weary with hearing of defeat after defeat. Then things began to change.

Reports of Union victories in Kentucky and Tennessee began to come in to the President. To celebrate, Mrs. Lincoln planned a grand party in the White House. The U.S. Marine Band played while the guests danced.

But the Lincolns didn't enjoy their party because their son Willie was very sick. In the middle of the evening, Mrs. Lincoln and the President went to check on their son. Fear filled their hearts when they saw how high the boy's temperature had climbed.

Soon, the Lincolns' younger son Tad became sick too. The boys both had a dangerous disease called typhoid fever. The President spent his nights sitting up with the two boys. He thought about all the happy times they'd shared, playing together at their home place in Springfield and at the White House.

> "The Lord is always on the side of the right. My real concern is that I and this nation should be on the Lord's side."
> President Abraham Lincoln

During the next two weeks, Willie grew worse and finally died. The Lincolns were heartbroken, and Mrs. Lincoln collapsed. For the next three weeks, she didn't leave her bedroom. It was a terrible time for everyone in the White House. Although Tad was getting better, the Lincolns felt like they would never laugh again.

President Lincoln cried often because he missed Willie, but he took comfort in the thought of his son enjoying a place where there was no war.

While the Lincolns tried to get over their personal tragedy, bad news often came from the battle front. The President and his top general weren't getting along with each other, and the war looked like it would go on for a long time.

Lincoln pushed toward a speedy victory, but nothing seemed to work. "I am almost ready to say that this war is God's will and that He's not ready for it to end yet," Lincoln wrote one day. "It is quite possible that God's purpose is something different from the purpose of either side in this battle."

Wondering what that purpose might be, Lincoln spent more and more time praying and reading the Bible. When his old friend Joshua Speed visited, he saw Lincoln with his Bible open. "I guess you have recovered from your religious doubts, but I haven't," Speed said.

Lincoln looked up at his friend with concern and said, "Take all of this Book you can understand, and take the rest on faith, and you will live and die a happier and better man."

At the beginning of the Civil War, President Lincoln had only intended to stop slavery from spreading into new U.S. territories and states. He believed slavery was wrong, but he also thought the Constitution made it illegal for him to force the Southern states to end it. He was sure slavery would eventually end in the South just as it had in the North.

As the war continued, President Lincoln's ideas changed. He decided that God wanted him to set all the slaves free. Once that decision was made, he began to act with greater confidence and direction.

On September 22, 1862, after the Union Army won the battle at Antietam, Lincoln told his advisors, "I made a solemn promise to God that if General Lee were driven back from Pennsylvania, I would celebrate the victory with the declaration of freedom to the slaves." Then he read the Emancipation Proclamation he had been writing and rewriting for many months.

★ ★ ★ ★ ★ ★

Today the place where the Battle of Gettysburg was fought is a national military park. The speech President Lincoln gave to honor the thousands of men who died at Gettysburg is engraved on the Lincoln Memorial in Washington, D.C. He said, "It is for us, the living, to dedicate ourselves to the unfinished work which they who fought here have so bravely advanced . . . Let us make sure that these dead shall not have died in vain—that this nation, under God, shall have a new birth of freedom—and that government of the people, by the people, for the people, shall not perish from the earth."

By then, President Lincoln thought of himself as a tool in God's hand. He said, "I have my opinions and my convictions of duty. But I am aware at every moment that all I am and all I have is subject to a Higher Power. That Power can use me or not use me in any way, and at any time, as it pleases Him."

When the war went on into 1863, Lincoln asked all Americans to spend a day in fasting and prayer. "Since we know that nations are subject to God's correction, we must consider that this awful civil war may be a punishment for our sins," he told them.

What were the sins of the nation? The President explained, "We have received the blessings of heaven, including many years of peace and prosperity. We have grown in numbers, wealth, and power as no other nation has ever grown. But we have forgotten God, and we have imagined that all these blessings were produced by our own superior goodness and wisdom. We have become too proud to pray to the God who made us!"

But there was still hope for America. Lincoln continued, "Let us trust that the united cry of the nation will be heard by God and answered with the forgiveness of our national sins and the return of our divided and suffering country to its past unity and peace."

The faith of the entire country was severely tested that summer when General Lee marched his troops into Pennsylvania. Just before the battle, President Lincoln went to his room and locked the door. Then he knelt to pray. "Lord, we can't stand another awful defeat like Fredericksburg or Chancellorsville," he said. Soon a feeling of comfort filled his heart. "It was as if God Almighty had taken the whole business into His own hands and that things would go all right at Gettysburg," he told a friend.

After three horrible days of fighting, the Confederate Army had to retreat. Although the Civil War continued almost two more years, the South never regained its strength. In gratitude for victory, President Lincoln set aside the last Thursday in November as a national day of thanksgiving.

As the war came to a close, Lincoln was elected to four more years as president. He asked the country to be firm in its stand for justice and truth, but to be kind to those who had fought against it. He wanted everyone to work together in binding up the nation's wounds and taking care of those who had suffered from the fighting.

President Lincoln didn't get to carry out his peace plans. John Wilkes Booth, a Southern actor who was outraged over Lincoln's decision to give African Americans the right to vote, shot the President. After leading the country he loved through its darkest and most dangerous time, this great man also gave his life for the cause of freedom.

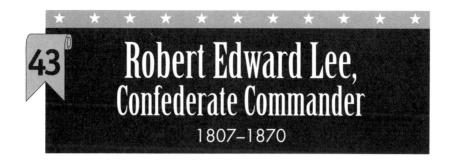

43 Robert Edward Lee, Confederate Commander
1807–1870

Young Lieutenant Robert E. Lee looked forward to his visits in the home of George Washington Parke Custis and his family. Their beautiful colonial house overlooked the Potomac River, and inside Lee felt like he had stepped back in time to visit the father of his country, George Washington. Mr. Custis was Washington's adopted son and enjoyed showing off Washington's personal belongings and telling stories about him.

Their daughter, Mary Anne, and Robert became sweethearts and decided to marry. Mr. and Mrs. Custis were delighted with their new son-in-law. "He's a brilliant young man, tops in his class at West Point," they told their friends. "In fact, he made it through his entire time at the Academy without ever breaking a single rule! Now he's part of the U.S. Army Corp of Engineers, building roads and bridges."

Today, the place where Robert E. Lee surrendered to U. S. Grant is a part of the Appomattox Court House National Historical Park. It looks much like it did the day of the surrender.

To show their happiness about Mary's choice of a husband, the Custises gave the young couple six of their slaves. Lee politely accepted the gift, but when he and Mary were alone he said, "I won't have slaves. I've hated slavery all my life. As my Uncle Richard Henry Lee once said, 'Slavery is wicked and shameful.' If he'd had his way at the Continental Congress almost a hundred years ago, things would be different now."

"Well, you must not go against your conscience," Mary said. And so they set the six slaves free immediately. Many years later, when Mr. Custis

died, he left orders for all his slaves to be set free. His son-in-law, Robert E. Lee, was delighted to carry out his wish.

When Abraham Lincoln became president, Colonel Lee was serving as commander in Texas, far from his Virginia home. But it didn't take long for news to reach him that the United States was tearing apart. On December 20, 1860, South Carolina declared itself independent from the Union. Soon Mississippi, Florida, Alabama, Georgia, Louisiana, and Texas followed. Lee feared Virginia would join its Southern neighbors.

Lee didn't commit himself to either side. In a private letter, he wrote, "As an American citizen, I take great pride in my country. But I can imagine no greater disaster for the country than for the Union to dissolve. Secession is nothing but revolution. But if the Union is dissolved, I will return to Virginia and share the miseries of my people."

In Arlington, Virginia, the home place of the Lee family is now part of the Arlington National Cemetery. The Union government took his mansion and 200 acres for use as a cemetery for Union soldiers.

Lee's fears came true in April 1861 when Confederate troops attacked Fort Sumter. The war between the states had begun, and Virginia joined the Confederate States of America. *What shall I do now?* Lee wondered as he fought back tears.

All night long he paced the floor in his home at Arlington, Virginia. Feeling overwhelmed with his decision, he knelt and prayed. "Lord, help me make this terrible choice. I have served my country for over thirty years and I don't want to turn my back on it now. I still believe slavery is evil. But I don't see how I can fight against my state, my relatives, and my neighbors." By morning, he had decided that he could not turn his back on Virginia. He resigned from the United States Army.

Jefferson Davis, President of the Confederate States, was delighted to have a brilliant military man like Lee on his side. He made Lee a general and put him in charge of the Army of Northern Virginia.

Lee and his troops won victory after victory. But Lee was miserable. "Oh, Mary, what a cruel thing war is," he wrote his wife on Christmas day after winning the battle of Fredericksburg. "It separates and destroys families and friends, and it spoils the purest joys God has given us. War fills our hearts with hatred instead of love for our neighbors, and it devastates the face of this beautiful world!"

In spite of Lee's brilliant battle plans and his soldiers' brave fighting, the war began to go in favor of the North. The South simply didn't have enough men or money to carry on with a long war. And no matter how many times General Lee won, President Lincoln wouldn't give up the fight to bring the Southern states back into the Union.

Lee knew there wasn't much hope of winning the war, but that wasn't his main concern. "Soldiers! Let us humble ourselves before the Lord, our God, asking through Christ, the forgiveness of our sins, and the aid of God in defending our homes and our liberties."

To the folks at home, he wrote, "Prayer is our mightiest weapon, so I plead with our people everywhere to pray. Let there be prayer at sunup, at noonday, at sundown, at midnight. Let us pray for our children, our elderly, our pastors, our homes, our churches, our nation. Let us pray for those who have never known Jesus Christ and redeeming love."

★ ★ ★ ★ ★ ★

Robert E. Lee and his family are buried at the Lee Chapel at Washington College (now Washington and Lee University) in Lexington, Virginia.

When General Lee visited with his son during a furlough, he complained about Jefferson Davis and the Confederate Congress. "They don't seem able to do anything except eat peanuts, chew tobacco, and make flowery speeches while my soldiers starve!" Lee said with anger. "When this war began I was bitterly opposed to it, and I told these people that unless every man should do his whole duty, they would regret it. But every state is determined to do only what it thinks is best for it alone."

Lee went on with the fighting the best he could, but his men were so weak from hunger they could scarcely stand up. General Grant, commander of the Northern Army, urged Lee to surrender. "What do you think, men?" Lee asked the other commanders. "Not yet!" they said. Lee agreed to hold out a little longer. He was worried about how Grant would treat the Southern troops if Lee surrendered.

Lee led his men toward Appomattox Court House, a little village with a railroad depot. He was counting on the arrival of supply trains so he could feed his soldiers. Before he could get there, the Northern troops captured the trains.

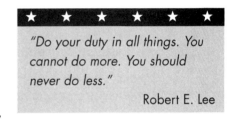

"Do your duty in all things. You cannot do more. You should never do less."

Robert E. Lee

On Palm Sunday, five years after the war had begun, General Lee surrendered to General Grant. The two men met in a farm house and Lee got what he most wanted—his soldiers would be allowed to go home to their families instead of being held prisoners.

Lee returned to his men and said, "We have fought through the war together. I have done my best for you. Now it is time to go home and take whatever work you find. Accept conditions as you find them. Consider only the present and the future. Do not hold onto bitterness."

After the war ended, Robert E. Lee became president of Washington College in Lexington, Virginia. It had been almost destroyed during the War, so it didn't have much to offer him. But he liked the idea of helping to rebuild a school named after his hero George Washington. He also wanted to help young Southerners rebuild their lives and their states.

Often people would say ugly things about the Union to Lee, thinking he would agree. He never did. Instead he told them, "Love your enemies. Even during the war, there was never a day I didn't pray for them."

As his life of duty and honor came to a close, Lee had only one wish. "If I could only know that all the young men in this college were good Christians," he told a visiting minister, "I should have nothing more to desire."

44

Clara Harlowe Barton,
Angel of the Battlefield
1821–1912

When President Lincoln called for Army volunteers, a quiet, fragile-looking clerk in the U.S. Patent Office thought, *Oh, how I wish I could enlist! If there were only something I could do to help my country.* But in 1861, there wasn't any place in a war for women.

Clara had a chance to get involved in the war effort sooner than she expected. She heard that a regiment from her home state of Massachusetts had been attacked on their way through Baltimore to Washington, D.C. Clara rushed to the train station to meet them. "Miss Barton!" a young man's voice called out. "Is that really you?"

Clara turned to see a former student, all grown up, in a military uniform. She greeted him and began asking questions about his regiment. Several of the men had attended the school where Clara once taught. Others were neighbors of her family. She learned that the soldiers had lost all their baggage in Baltimore, so she quickly went to work, gathering supplies for them.

When Clara and five black porters carried big baskets of food, handkerchiefs, towels, string, soap, and other important items into the Senate room where the Massachusetts regiment was staying, the men cheered. "Well, you're my boys," Clara told them. "I had to do something."

That night Clara couldn't sleep. She kept thinking about the soldiers and their many needs. She knew the Army wouldn't supply the things they'd lost. *I know, I'll write a letter to the Worcester, Massachusetts, newspaper*, she thought. *Surely, the mothers, sisters, wives, and girlfriends of these men will want to help.*

Sure enough, packages began arriving soon after Clara's letter appeared in the paper. She received the boxes with joy, but they created a new problem for her. *Where can I keep all these things until I can get them to those in need?* she wondered. *And how will I find the time to pass out all that's been given?*

Always a good planner and organizer, Clara found someone to take her job at the patent office. Then she rented an apartment in the downtown business section of the nation's capitol. She took a small part of the large room, and the rest quickly filled with donations for the Union soldiers.

In the summer of 1861, the Union and Confederate troops met for their first great battle near a stream called Bull Run, in Manassas, Virginia. Since the battlefield wasn't far from Washington, D.C., many of the politicians and their wives went there by carriage to watch the fighting. Everyone expected a quick victory for the Union. Instead, they saw a horrible defeat. Hundreds of dead and wounded soldiers covered the battle ground.

When the fighting was over, the Union Army sent its 1,000 wounded men up the Potomac River. They lay in the hot sun on the Washington docks because there wasn't room in the hospitals for them. Clara rushed to see what she could do for the soldiers. She moved a few of the men into her apartment and nursed them. She also visited those left on the docks every day.

"These men should have received care on the battlefield," Clara told her sister Sally. "Why should they be left untended when they're giving their lives for us?" Tears threatened to spill down her cheeks.

"My kindhearted Clara," Sally said. "You're doing all you can."

"No, I want to go to the camps," Clara said. "Perhaps I can get other women to go and help, too."

"You're dreaming, Clara!" Sally said in alarm. "They would never let a woman go to the front lines of the fighting."

"I will find a way," Clara said with determination. "It is where I am needed most."

For the next year, Clara tried to persuade officials to let her do nursing on the battlefields. Finally, the U.S. Surgeon General agreed. He handed her written orders to show to the military commanders. Clara read with excitement, "Miss C.H. Barton has permission to go on the sick transports in any direction—for the purpose of distributing comforts for the sick and wounded and nursing them—always subject to the direction of the doctor in charge."

Clara secured an Army wagon, mule team, and driver, loaded up with supplies, and headed for the battlefield. When she arrived at Cedar Mountain, cannon shells were bursting all around. "Show me to your hospital tent," Clara told an astonished young soldier.

Dr. Dunn welcomed the bandages and other supplies but wondered what to do with Clara. When he saw how well she went about caring for the wounded soldiers, he decided she was just what they needed. By the end of the first day, the men were calling her their angel—the Angel of the Battlefield.

For the next three years of the Civil War, Clara Barton did without sleep and lived a rugged life in the fields in order to serve her country. She built fires in rainy weather, cooked soup and hot cereal for the sick and wounded, applied bandages, sat with dying soldiers, wrote letters for them, recruited other nurses, and gathered supplies. When she became tired and sick, she rested a while and then hurried back to her work.

A worried friend said, "Clara, you are so small and frail. How do you stand to see so much blood and suffering?"

"By forgetting myself," Clara answered. "That is the only way. You must never think of anything but the need and how to meet it. Then God gives the strength and the thing that seemed impossible is done."

★ ★ ★ ★ ★ ★

To better understand the Angel of the Battlefield and the work of the American Red Cross, visit the Clara Barton House in Glen Echo, Maryland, near Washington, D.C. Once a warehouse, it became Clara's home and headquarters of the Red Cross in 1897. This National Historic Site contains fascinating photos and papers, explaining Clara's work. Costumed guides tell the amazing story of this great American woman.

Just before the War ended, Clara wrote President Lincoln to ask for a new job. She wanted to help find the thousands of soldiers who were missing. He agreed, but Clara had to use her own savings account of $15,000 to pay for her expenses. For four years, she worked to identify men in unmarked graves and prisoner of war camps.

By 1869, Clara was completely exhausted and very ill. Her doctor told her to go to Europe in order to get completely away from her work. During her trip, Clara learned about the work of the International Association of the Red Cross. She was thrilled to learn that countries had joined together in providing help on battlefields and wherever disasters happened. She spent two years working with the Red Cross in Germany and then came home to get Americans involved in this wonderful new organization.

After eight years of talking to U.S. leaders, Clara Barton achieved her goal. The American chapter of the Red Cross was born. Clara served as its president until 1904, bringing help to victims of floods, fires, hurricanes, epidemics, and wars.

When asked the reason for her life of public service, Clara quoted some words of Jesus from the Bible: "'Inasmuch as you have done it unto the least of these my brothers, you have done it unto me.'" Then she said, "I never did a day's work at the field that was not built on that one little sentence. It came into my mind hourly until sleep brought relief to my body and mind."

45

Hiram Revels,
First African American Senator
1827–1901

Much of the South lay in ruins after the Civil War. Many of its homes, churches, and schools had been destroyed during the fighting. The rest had suffered from years of neglect while Southern men were serving in the Confederate Army. The end of slavery also brought many changes in the way people lived and worked.

At first, every Southern state was under the control of the U.S. Army. In order to govern themselves once again, states like Mississippi had to write new constitutions that guaranteed the loyalty of its citizens to the United States government. They also had to promise equal treatment for blacks and whites.

In 1870, almost five years after the Civil War ended, Mississippi set up a new state government. For the first time, black men had a place in the state legislature. Some of those elected had been slaves, but others were free men like Reverend Hiram Revels of Natchez.

Although he wanted to serve his country and his people, Rev. Revels shook his head when folks urged him to get involved in government. "I don't want politics to get in the way of my work as a minister of the Gospel," he said. "And my color will no doubt cause many people to disapprove." But after talking with trusted friends, he agreed to become an city councilman.

Because of his gentle, peace-loving attitude and his intelligence, Revels found that most Mississippi folks respected him. He carefully kept his political work separate from his church work. Soon the people of

Adams County elected him to represent them in the Mississippi State Senate. Then, in January 1870, something incredible happened. Hiram Revels was appointed to the United States Senate. "You'll be sitting in the President's seat, Hiram," one of his friends told him.

Rev. Revels laughed. "Yes, I suppose I will be," he said. "Sittin' in the seat of poor old President Jefferson Davis of the Confederate States of America. Imagine that! Well, I hope I do my country a better service than he did!"

When Rev. Revels arrived in Washington, D.C., he discovered that some of the senators didn't want him there. "How could a colored man be qualified for this job?" they asked themselves. Although Revels was a loyal Republican like them and had done his part in the war effort, he quickly learned most white people still didn't think African Americans were their equals. For three long days, they looked at his history and talked about whether he was worthy to serve in the Senate. Here's what they learned about this quiet, dignified Methodist minister:

Beginning with Rev. Hiram Revels, many African Americans have served in Congress. In 1966, Edward Brooke of Massachusetts became the first black man elected to the Senate by popular vote.

Born to free parents in North Carolina, Revels had attended Quaker schools in Indiana. After graduating from Knox College in Ohio, he began his work as a preacher, pastor, and educator. For a while he traveled and preached to African Americans in several states. Then he moved to Baltimore, Maryland, where he pastored a Presbyterian church and served as a school principal.

When the Civil War began, Rev. Revels encouraged black men to form their own army regiments and fight for the Union. During the War, he moved to St. Louis and started a school for freed slaves. In 1864, he became the chaplain of a regiment of freedmen from Mississippi. Two years later, he decided to make his home in Natchez, Mississippi. During the four years before Rev. Revels went to Washington, he had been doing everything he could to help rebuild his adopted city and state.

Senator Charles Sumner, a brave friend of African Americans, stood up to speak for Hiram Revels. He convinced the Senate to accept Revels. But many hard battles lay ahead. When Rev. Revels was invited to speak at a meeting in Philadelphia, the city refused to let him speak in its Academy of Music because of his skin color. The battle against slavery was over, but the war for equal rights had just begun.

As white Southerners watched black people take honored places in society, they became afraid that African Americans would take over their jobs and property. Some of them burned the homes and businesses of black people. Others accused the black men serving in a government of misrule and robbery.

★ ★ ★ ★ ★ ★

Black churches have encouraged their members to take an active part in American politics, especially voting. Several African American ministers have served in Congress, including Andrew Young, Walter Fauntroy, William Gray III, and J.C. Watts. Other Christian ministers such as Martin Luther King, Ralph Abernathy, and Jesse Jackson have influenced American politics and government through their speeches, writing, and peaceful demonstrations.

Senator Revels spoke up for African Americans in the forty-first Congress. "The past record of my race is a true sign of their feelings today. They bear no revengeful thoughts or hatred toward their former masters," he said. "They do not aim to raise themselves by taking away any benefits of the white citizens. They ask only for the rights which are theirs by God's universal law, and which are the natural result of the freedom this nation has given them." He paused and looked around the Senate chamber, calling on every politician to do what was right. "They appeal to you and to me to see that they receive that protection which alone will let them go about their daily work with success and enjoy the liberties of citizenship the same as their white neighbors and friends."

Revels proved to be a capable senator. He supported new laws that would give back white Southerners' rights to vote and serve in government jobs. "The best way for colored people to gain their rightful place in America is not by violence, but by getting an education and leading clean, courageous lives," he told his people.

During his year in Washington, D.C., Senator Revels spoke out against the city's segregated school system and the Washington Navy Yard, which refused jobs to African American men.

After serving his short term in the Senate, Rev. Revels returned to pastor in Mississippi and also became president of Alcorn College. He stayed active in state government and surprised everyone by helping to remove Northern Republicans from control of the state. But Hiram Revels' first love was always Christian ministry. In fact, he spent the last happy hours of his life in church!

46 James Garfield,
Preacher Who Became President
1831–1881

I'm going to leave this Ohio farm and go to sea, James Garfield thought to himself. He swung an ax hard, splitting a piece of wood and sending it flying across the yard. But the closest he could come to his dream right now was running errands for the canal boat captains in nearby Cleveland, or reading stories about men who sailed the ocean.

That night, Jim told his mother, "I'll never be a farmer like Pa was. I think one of the ship captains in Cleveland will hire me for his crew, and I'm ready to go."

Mrs. Garfield frowned. "You're only sixteen and I want you to get an education. You were born to be great and good, not to be a rough sailor."

"Ma, you know I love books, but I'm getting too old for the little school here and we don't have money for me to go anywhere else."

The next morning James Garfield said good-bye to his family and walked to Cleveland. Instead of getting on a ship, he had to take a job on the canal. After six weeks of hard work, he became sick. Unhappily, he went home.

"You're burning up with fever, Jimmy," his mother said when he reached the cabin. She put him to bed and bathed his face with cool water. For the next four months, James was very sick. Often he heard his mother praying that he would get well, and finally he did.

"Jimmy, the Lord has spared your life for a reason," Mrs. Garfield said. "I have seventeen dollars, and I want you to take it and go to the Baptist academy."

James agreed. "I promise I'll pay you back, Ma," he said. "And I promise to make something out of my life."

At Geauga Academy, James Garfield fell in love with learning and forgot about going to sea. He also came to share his mother's strong faith in God and was baptized into the church known as the Disciples of Christ.

The tall, handsome, athletic young man studied hard and became a teacher. People often complimented him on his speaking and his clear thinking. "You would make a fine preacher, Jim," they told him. Soon he was preaching every Sunday in nearby churches. He gave lively and convincing sermons, calling on people to repent of their sins and put their faith in Jesus Christ. Many of them did.

Because of his strong religious beliefs, James decided to continue his education at a Disciples of Christ school called Hiram College. Then, to learn more about how other people thought and believed, he went to Williams College in Massachusetts. During this time, he became deeply disturbed about slavery. He realized that sometimes Christians needed to get involved in politics and government in order to change things that were wrong.

★ ★ ★ ★ ★ ★

In Cleveland, Ohio, you can see the Garfield Monument at the Lake View Cemetery. At the bottom of the round tower is a square stone porch. The panels of the porch picture scenes from Garfield's life. Inside the memorial hall, you'll find a marble statue of the President standing in the light that comes through fourteen stained-glass windows— one for each original state and Garfield's home state of Ohio.

When he finished his studies at Williams, Garfield returned to Hiram College as a professor of Greek and Latin. At the age of twenty-six, he became the school's president. He also went on preaching every Sunday, and during the summers he held revival meetings in which he preached every evening. Sometimes he debated experts in religion and science.

One day some leaders in Ohio's Republican Party came to see Garfield. "Would you consider running for state senator?" they asked him. "We think you could win and do a good job. And as a state senator, you could help us in the fight against slavery." Garfield agreed and was elected.

When the Civil War began, James Garfield enlisted in the Union Army. His successes won him the rank of major general. Before the War ended, Ohio chose him as one of their representatives in Congress. During his seventeen years as a member of the House of Representatives, Garfield won a reputation as a great speaker, a smart politician, and a relentless fighter for what he believed was right. He voted for the Fifteenth Amendment, which gave African Americans full rights as U.S. citizens. He also investigated how the U.S. government used its money and tried to make sure it was spent wisely.

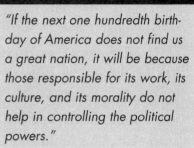

"If the next one hundredth birthday of America does not find us a great nation, it will be because those responsible for its work, its culture, and its morality do not help in controlling the political powers."

President James Garfield

One of the things that bothered Garfield the most was the way presidents and other politicians picked people for government jobs. They could choose anyone they wanted, even if that person had no training, ability, or honesty. He hoped someday he would be able to help create a better system.

In 1880, James Garfield had the biggest surprise of his life. After he gave a great speech at the Republican National Convention, the leaders decided to dump their candidate for president and have Garfield run instead. He won the election, and in March 1881 he became the nation's twentieth president.

As President Garfield talked about his hopes and plans for America, his eighty-year-old mother listened with pride. She whispered to her daughter-in-law, "He is the best son a mother ever had."

In the summer of his first year as president, Garfield decided to attend his class reunion at Williams College in Massachusetts. His sons Harry and Jim would travel with him and enroll in their father's school. On July 2, at the Washington train station, a crazy lawyer aimed a pistol at him and fired twice. He had been disappointed when the President didn't give him a government job

For the next two months, President Garfield tried to recover. But one of his wounds became infected. Just before he died, he heard church bells ringing.

"Are they praying for me?" he asked his doctor.

"Yes, the people of the entire country are praying for you today," the doctor said.

"God bless them!" President Garfield said. Eleven days later, he died. His family and his country were heartbroken. His death encouraged Congress to pass laws that protected politicians from people seeking government jobs. Just as Garfield had hoped, these jobs would now go to people who earned the right to have them.

James Garfield's life didn't go the way he had planned. When we wonder why bad things like his assassination happen, it's important to remember these words of President Garfield: "The world's history is a poem written by God. Although sometimes we are troubled by the sounds of cannon fire and the cries of dying men, the Christian can still hear the melody of God's song which speaks of hope and peaceful days to come."

Frances, why don't you stay home with your mother today, instead of going hunting with Oliver," Mr. Willard said. "It's time you learned to behave like a girl."

Her sunny faced turned into a storm cloud, but Frances knew better than to disobey her father. *If I hurry with the housework, maybe I can still go hunting later,* she thought. *Why should boys get to have all the adventures?* she wondered. *It's not fair.* As her father walked out the door, she daringly said, "I'll do as you say, Father, but you must call me Frank in return."

Mr. Willard smiled at his tomboy and said, "All right, Frank."

While Frances swept the floor, she dreamed of riding horseback across the fields of her family's Wisconsin homestead, through the woods, and over the western mountains. Next to being outdoors, she loved reading adventure stories about the Wild West or pirate tales from the sea. She always pictured herself as the bravest, most adventurous person in the story.

"Mother, may I please go now?" Frances asked after a couple of hours at her chores.

"Yes, dear," Mrs. Willard said. "It's my belief we should let a girl grow as a tree grows—according to her own sweet nature. Have a good time with Oliver. And be careful!"

In 1860, after her graduation from college, Frances started teaching. As the years went by she became an excellent teacher and a person of great

honesty and courage. She also enjoyed writing and had many articles published in newspapers and magazines. Always eager for new adventures, "Frank" traveled with a friend to Europe. When she returned to her home in Evanston, Illinois, she received an invitation to become president of a brand new school—the Evanston Ladies College. The college would be part of Northwestern University, but Frances Willard would have complete control.

"At last I am free to follow my own course as an elder sister of girls," Frances told a friend after becoming head of the women's school. Every afternoon, Miss Willard talked to all the students about growing a life of kindness, honesty, loyalty, and other good qualities. The students loved these times since she talked to them as her friends, rather than preaching at them. Often Miss Willard visited her students in their rooms and led them in evening prayers.

In 1873, the new president and board of Northwestern University forced Miss Willard to give up her successful work as head of the women's college. They didn't think a woman should have such an important job. Heartbroken, Frances taught English and art in the university for a year. But some of the male students made her life miserable. Day after day, they pulled pranks on her. She didn't lose her temper with these mean students or with the University's leaders, but when summer came she left Northwestern.

★ ★ ★ ★ ★ ★

In 1905, the State of Illinois placed a statue of Frances E. Willard in Statuary Hall in Washington, D.C. It shows her standing to speak, as she often did. In her hand, she holds the notes for her speech about the need to give women the right to vote.

One day, she received a letter from the Women's Christian Temperance Union (WCTU), a group that had declared war on the liquor business. Frances had often read about their Crusade in the newspaper. Reports said that in less than two months, these brave women had closed down saloons and bars in over 200 towns. This was wonderful news, especially since drinking had become an extremely serious problem in the years following the Civil War.

Now the Chicago branch needed a new president. "It has come to me, as I believe from the Lord, that you ought to be our president," the letter said.

After praying about it and reading her Bible, Frances believed she knew what to do. She said, "yes" to the women's crusade against alcohol.

Instead of teaching university students, Miss Willard marched down Chicago's streets with other sisters, mothers, and wives. The police ordered the women not to block the way of other people, but they could gather along the curb in front of bars and stores that sold liquor. No matter how people laughed or attacked them, they were determined to stop the terrible effects of drinking on American families.

★ ★ ★ ★ ★ ★

Miss Willard learned how to ride a bicycle at the age of fifty-three and enjoyed it tremendously. Always on the go, she said, "Proverbs tells us that 'The wicked flee when no man pursues.' It is also true that they make better time when someone is after them!" Frances Willard kept after them all of her life.

One day on Market Street, just outside Sheffner's saloon, the women began to sing a Christian hymn as they usually did. Frances Willard joined in. As they sang, beer wagons rumbled down the stone paved street. An elderly woman passing by said, "God bless you girls for doing this. I lost my son to drink, so I know what you're doing is right." The woman knelt on the street and prayed for the Women's Crusade.

Then the ladies walked into the barroom. One of them read from the Bible and together they sang another hymn. At first the men in the bar called out rude remarks. But when Frances and the other women knelt in the sawdust that covered the floor, the saloon became silent. Tears came to the eyes of tough men as they thought about their families. Many of them decided to quit drinking because of the women's courageous actions.

Miss Willard found great satisfaction in her work with the Women's Christian Temperance Union. In 1879, she was asked to put her many skills to work as president of the national organization. From then on, much of her time was spent traveling and speaking to groups of women throughout the United States.

One morning during a trip to Ohio, Frances knelt to pray alone in her room. Into her mind and heart came a new direction. "You are to speak for a women's right to vote as a way of protecting homes and loved ones from the cruel effects of drinking." She believed the thought came from God.

Under Miss Willard's leadership, the WCTU adopted two slogans: first, "For God and Home and Native Land," and second, "Do everything!" The women prepared textbooks and teaching materials for schools and churches, opened boys' clubs, taught girls about health and homemaking, started homes for alcoholic women, fought against the growing problem of drugs, and tried to convince everyone—especially government leaders—that drinking was bad for the person, the family, and the country.

When Frances Willard became president of the WCTU, it had only a few hundred members. Less than twenty years later, it had 200,000 adult members and almost as many youth members. In 1891, the WCTU became a worldwide group, strong enough to influence politicians. Instead of training a few hundred young women, God had opened the door for Frances Willard to shape Americans' beliefs and behavior for many years to come.

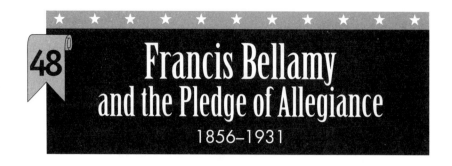

48 Francis Bellamy and the Pledge of Allegiance
1856–1931

How can we help children celebrate the 400th anniversary of Columbus' discovery in a special way?" James Upham, editor of *The Youth's Companion* magazine, asked his assistant.

"Hmm," Francis Bellamy said, thinking hard. "I suppose it should really be a celebration of America. Maybe we could do something with the U.S. flag."

"Good idea," Upham said. His eyes began to sparkle with excitement. "We could have the children raise money to buy flags for their schools."

"I would be glad to write a pledge or salute to the flag that the children could repeat," said Bellamy. He was a Baptist minister and writer, so he had a talent for using words in creative ways.

"All right," Upham agreed. "But make it short and easy to remember."

When Rev. Bellamy started working on the pledge to the flag, he discovered how hard it was to put big ideas into just a few words. He wrote pledge after pledge, but they all wound up in the trash can.

One day he rushed into Upham's office. He waved a paper and said, "I think I've got it! Listen to this:

I pledge allegiance to my flag
and to the republic for which it stands:
one nation, indivisible,
with liberty and justice for all.

Upham agreed it was a great pledge. "But will children understand what it means?" he asked.

"Well, you did tell me to keep it short, and you'll notice it contains just twenty-three words," Rev. Bellamy said. "We can write an explanation in the magazine when we print the pledge to the flag."

"And how would you explain *allegiance*?" Upham asked.

"It's a promise to be true to our country. It means we'll do whatever it takes to protect it and keep it strong and healthy," said Rev. Bellamy.

"How about *republic*?" Upham said. He enjoyed testing his assistant writer-editor.

"America is a republic because it has leaders who are chosen by its people," Bellamy answered.

"What about *indivisible*?" Upham said.

Bellamy fired back the answer. "Unable to be broken apart. Our Civil War proved that the states are one united body. It also won liberty for everyone in America."

Upham smiled and said, "Good job, Bellamy!"

On September 8, 1892, *The Youth's Companion* published the pledge. It also explained how students could take part in honoring the flag. Soon letters from all over the country came pouring into the magazine office.

The flag of the United States is sometimes called "The Stars and Stripes," "Old Glory," or the "Red, White, and Blue." The Continental Congress explained the meaning of the colors in our flag in this way: "White stands for purity and innocence; red stands for hardiness and valor; and blue stands for vigilance, perseverance and justice."

"I will ask my teacher to let us repeat the pledge on Columbus Day," hundreds of children wrote. Teachers also wrote to the magazine, thanking its editors for encouraging children to help purchase flags. They welcomed the pledge, too, and promised to help their students understand exactly what it meant.

On Columbus Day, October 21, 1892, Rev. Bellamy listened as 6,000 Boston children said the pledge together. On the same day, students in big cities, little towns, and one-room country schools were also saluting the U.S. flag. And at the World's Fair in Chicago, thousands of Americans of all ages recited the new pledge. There were many wonderful things to see and do at the Fair, but many thought the pledge to the flag was the best of all.

Almost immediately, Rev. Bellamy's twenty-three words became an important part of America's traditions. Instead of saying the pledge only on Columbus Day, people began to repeat it at important gatherings. Eventually, students in all our public schools and most private schools said the pledge each day.

In 1949, President Harry S. Truman and Congress created Flag Day. You can join other Americans in celebrating on June 14 by flying a flag in front of your home or attending a Flag Day parade in your city.

Since 1892 Rev. Bellamy's words have only been changed twice. In 1923, the National Flag Conference of the American Legion—a group of men who had been soldiers—decided that people should say exactly which flag they were saluting. They changed the words to "I pledge allegiance to the flag of the United States of America." They also asked Americans to place their right hands on their hearts. It was one more way of showing that a serious promise was being made.

A year later, in 1924, the U.S. Congress voted to make the Pledge of Allegiance our official salute to the flag. From then on, no one but our nation's lawmakers could change it.

In 1954, on the fiftieth birthday of Rev. Bellamy's pledge, one congressman suggested adding two important words to the pledge—"under God." He reminded everyone of how Abraham Lincoln called the United States "one nation under God" in his most famous speech. Congress voted to make the change, and President Dwight Eisenhower agreed. He said, "In this way we are declaring the importance of religious faith in America's heritage and future." By repeatedly remembering America's dependence on God's help and protection, President Eisenhower believed "we shall constantly strengthen those spiritual weapons which forever will be our country's most powerful resource in peace and war."

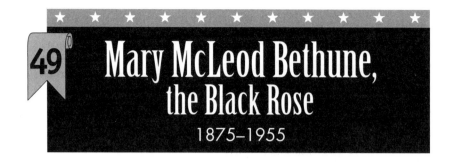

Mary McLeod Bethune, the Black Rose
1875–1955

On her first day in the Presbyterian mission school, seven-year-old Mary McLeod (mac-loud) had to pinch herself to make sure she wasn't dreaming. No one in her whole family had ever been to school. There were no public schools for African American children in most Southern towns. But thanks to some generous Christians, Mayesville, South Carolina, had a school and a black teacher named Miss Emma Wilson.

Mary could hardly wait to begin learning to read. She watched in fascination as Miss Wilson opened the Bible. "Children, listen to what God's Son said about His Father's love for you," the teacher said. "God so loved the world that He gave His one and only Son, that whoever believes in Him shall not perish but have eternal life."

Miss Wilson looked up at her students and said, "That word 'whoever' means you. No matter what others may say about you, you are just as important and loved by God as anyone else in the whole world. And the Lord wants you to learn."

Mary McLeod had never heard such an amazing thing. But her parents had taught her to believe in God, Jesus, and the Bible. She thought, *If God said it, it must be true.* From that moment on, Mary McLeod believed she was somebody.

Each day in the little schoolhouse brought new adventures: learning to read and count; hearing new stories from the Bible; and, studying history, geography, and the wonders of nature. Then, at the age of eleven, Mary completed all the studies Miss Wilson offered. Her family came to

watch her graduate, proud and excited that their first child to be born free from slavery had an education, too.

For the next year, Mary worked in the cotton fields all day. Whenever her father went to sell his cotton or pay his bills, Mary went along to do the counting for him. At night she taught her brothers and sisters what she had learned in school, and she read to her family from the Bible. She missed going to school, and she prayed, "Lord, make a way for me to go on learning."

You can learn more about this incredible woman by visiting the Bethune Museum in Washington, D.C. or Bethune-Cookman College in Daytona Beach, Florida.

One day Miss Wilson came to visit the McLeods. "I have good news," she said. Her face glowed with happiness. "A seamstress in Colorado has offered to pay for one of my students to go on to another school." She looked at Mary and smiled. "I chose you, Mary. If your parents think it is all right, you can attend Scotia Seminary where I studied."

"Scotia?" Mary's mother asked. She looked happy and worried all at once.

"It's a Christian school for black girls in Concord, North Carolina," Miss Wilson said. "After Mary finishes the general studies, she can also learn to be a teacher at Scotia if she wants to."

"Oh, yes!" Mary said. And her parents agreed.

Four years later Mary graduated from Scotia Seminary. None of her family had the money to come and see her receive her diploma. But she had many wonderful school friends to share her joy. And thanks to Miss Chrissman, the woman who paid her school bills, Mary could go on studying four more years in the Scotia school for teachers.

In 1894 Mary completed her training as a teacher. For some time she had dreamed of going to teach in Africa. In her letters to Miss Chrissman, Mary wrote about her longing to tell Africans about God's love.

Miss Chrissman wrote back and said, "How would you like to go to Moody Bible Institute in Chicago, Illinois, for a year of missionary training? I'll be glad to pay your way."

Nineteen-year-old Miss Mary McLeod eagerly enrolled. She was the only black in the large Chicago school. She enjoyed her time at Moody Institute, but her dream of going to Africa was crushed. The Mission Board told her, "We have no openings for Negro missionaries to Africa."

Instead of letting her disappointment defeat her, Mary decided to teach African Americans. "Neither God nor man can use a discouraged person," she said. And more than anything, she wanted to be useful. As a young teacher, she married Albertus Bethune (buh-thoon) and had a little boy she named Albert.

After several years of teaching in South Carolina, Georgia, and Florida, Mrs. Bethune decided to start a school of her own. Many black people had moved to Daytona Beach to help build a railroad for tourists. Their children needed a school.

Mrs. Bethune found a run-down four-room house to rent, got the neighbors to help her fix it up, and started her school. She and her students used wooden boxes for desks and chairs, berry juice for ink, and burned logs to make charcoal for pencils. Mrs. Bethune sold pies and went door-to-door asking for donations to her school. When folks heard her beautiful voice and saw her handsome, loving face, many of them eagerly gave money to help.

In 1974, a statue of Mary McLeod Bethune was dedicated in a Washington, D.C. park. It shows her handing a paper to a boy and a girl. At the bottom of the statue, visitors can read Mrs. Bethune's last words: "I leave you faith, I leave you hope, I leave you love."

In just two years, Mrs. Bethune's school had grown from five students to 250. Although she was still very poor, Mrs. Bethune believed God would help her build a school big enough for all the students who wanted to come. And, somehow, He did. The new school building was named Faith Hall. As they walked into the building, students read the words, "Enter to learn." As they walked out, they read, "Depart to serve."

Mrs. Bethune compared the different kinds of people in the world to flowers in a garden. "In the people garden there are red and yellow, tiny and tall," she said. "Although each flower is different, each is beautiful."

"But Mrs. Bethune, there's no place in the people garden for blacks," a girl once said. "There's no such thing as a black flower."

"Ah, child, just because you haven't seen one doesn't mean there is no such thing," Mrs. Bethune answered.

On a visit to Europe, Mrs. Bethune found out how right she had been. In Holland, she received black tulips. And in Switzerland friends showed her the black rose. "I want seventy of those wonderful rose bushes to plant outside my school!" she said with delight.

In time, Mary McLeod Bethune's school became Bethune-Cookman College. She also founded the National Council of Negro Women, served in important federal government positions, and worked in many ways to improve the lives of African Americans.

50 Katherine Lee Bates and America's Favorite Song
1859–1929

"All aboard!" called the train conductor, and passengers began crowding into the railroad cars. Miss Katherine Bates felt a rush of excitement as her first journey west began. She had been tired from a busy year of writing and teaching at Wellesley College, a women's school near Boston. But the idea of seeing the World's Fair in Chicago, the Rocky Mountains of Colorado, and teaching a special summer school gave her fresh energy.

"I wouldn't miss this adventure for the world!" the jolly Miss Bates told the colleagues that traveled with her. They nodded, looking forward to a month of new sights and experiences.

After a day and a half of sitting up in straight, hard train seats, the college professors cheered when they reached Chicago. They checked into a hotel, rested a while, and then headed for the World Colombian Exposition.

"Oh!" Katherine gasped when the fair grounds and its beautiful buildings came into view. She had read about the "White City" being built for the World's Fair and how it had cost more than $31,000,000. But nothing she had read prepared her for the gleaming alabaster halls and palaces she now saw. A reflection of the alabaster city shimmered on the water of nearby Lake Michigan. "It's like a dreamland out of the future," Katherine said in awe.

> Although Miss Bates did her best to make her poem easy to understand, you may need to look up some of the words. Ask a grown-up to help you understand what each verse means. Sing it together. You may want to draw pictures of each beauty in America that Katherine Bates described. Of course, the best way to understand her thoughts is to travel across America.

For the next several days, Katherine and her friends visited some of the 65,000 exhibits at the fair. They walked down America's first midway and tried not to lose each other in the crowds. The fair had new machines and inventions of all kinds, grand music, and interesting foods. "This is more fabulous than anything I saw in Europe," Katherine told her friends.

Soon it was time to get back on the train and continue the trip to Colorado. Katherine saw another kind of beauty on the trip—wonders made by God instead of men and women. The prairies spread out for hundreds of miles on either side of the train. Golden in the sunlight, they grew the grain for America's bread. An enormous blue sky stretched over the prairies.

As the train chugged west, the land rose toward the Rocky Mountains. Katherine and her friends stared out the train windows, too excited to speak. As the sunlight moved across the mountains, it painted them green, brown, and gold. Evening turned the same mountains to deep blue and purple. *This is the greatest masterpiece of all time!* Katherine thought.

When the train reached the lovely town of Colorado Springs, high in the Rocky Mountains, Katherine and the other teachers got off. For the next three weeks they stretched the minds of students at the new Colorado College. Katherine loved teaching young people to enjoy language and great books. Helping others learn was as exciting for her as sightseeing.

At night in her hotel room, Katherine

★ ★ ★ ★ ★ ★

If you go up Pike's Peak, think of Miss Bates and her prayer for our country. Interestingly, Colorado Springs at the foot of Pike's Peak is now the home of over ninety Christian ministries and more than 450 churches. It's definitely an inspiring place!

wrote about the many new things she had seen on her trip. She also wrote poems filled with strong feelings she couldn't find any other way to express. Her friends said she had a singing heart, always ready to overflow in poetry.

Just before the visit to Colorado ended, some of the professors said, "Let's take a trip up to Pike's Peak. We can't go back to Massachusetts without seeing the view from up there."

Katherine looked up at the mountain that towered thousands of feet above Colorado Springs. Although she was only thirty-four, she spent much of her time indoors teaching, reading, and writing. She couldn't imagine climbing a mountain. "How would we ever get up there?" she asked.

"Oh, it'll be easy," a friend said. "All we have to do is rent a prairie wagon and drive up as far as it can go. Then we'll ride mules the rest of the way. There will be guides to help us all the way."

It didn't sound at all easy to Katherine, but she didn't want to be left out of the fun. When the group reached the top, she didn't regret her decision.

"We're 14,000 feet above the ground," their guide said. "Up here, the air is very thin. That's why the sky looks like a blue sapphire."

Katherine drank in the beauty all around her—sky, mountain meadows, jagged rocky slopes, fields, and rivers. A song started deep within her.

O beautiful for spacious skies,
For amber waves of grain,
For purple mountain majesties
Above the fruited plain!
America! America!
God shed His grace on thee
And crown thy good with brotherhood
From sea to shining sea!

Before Katherine went to bed that night, she wrote down the words that had come into her mind. *What are some of the other beautiful things about America?* she asked herself. She thought of her father and grandfather, both ministers with a deep faith in God . . . her Pilgrim ancestors and their struggle for freedom . . . the soldiers who had given their lives in America's wars . . . the dreamers, builders, and inventors who were helping the nation move into a bright future.

As these thoughts flowed through her mind, she wrote.

O beautiful for pilgrim feet,
Whose stern, impassioned stress
A thoroughfare for freedom beat
Across the wilderness!
America! America!

God mend thine every flaw,
Confirm thy soul in self-control,
Thy liberty in law!

O beautiful for heroes proved
In liberating strife,
Who more than self their country loved,
And mercy more than life!
America! America!
May God thy gold refine
Till all success be nobleness
And every gain divine!

O beautiful for patriot dream
That sees beyond the years
Thine alabaster cities gleam
Undimmed by human tears!
America! America!
God shed His grace on thee
And crown thy good with brotherhood
From sea to shining sea!

When she finished, Katherine realized her poem had turned into a prayer for the country she loved. She closed her Colorado notebook and went to sleep dreaming of the view from Pike's Peak.

For two years, Katherine's poem stayed in her notebook. Then one day while reading about her trip to Colorado, she thought, *Perhaps I could help other people understand how wonderful America is by sharing my poem.* She mailed the poem to a Christian magazine called *The Congregationalist*.

On July 4, 1895, *America the Beautiful* appeared in print. People loved it and copied it to give to their friends. Some found tunes that fit the poem and began to sing Miss Bates' words. After changing it a few times to make it more simple and easy to remember, Katherine Lee Bates gave away her rights to the poem. In the early 1900s, it became America's best-loved song.

GLOSSARY

abolition—the complete destruction of something.

abolitionist—a person who wishes to do away with something, such as slavery.

acre—a measurement of land; somewhat smaller than a football field.

act of Congress—a law or decision made by Congress.

advisor—someone who helps others decide what they should do.

alabaster—smooth, white stone often used for carving.

Algonquins— (al gong'kwen) a group of Native American tribes from eastern Canada's Ottawa river valley; a family of languages spoken by Indian tribes in a large portion of America.

allegiance—a promise to be faithful to a country, government, group, or person.

Almighty—having more power than anyone else; God.

ambassador—a person sent to represent his or her country in talks with another government.

amendment—a change in or an addition to an existing law.

antislavery—against the practice of holding men, women, and children as if they were one's property.

archaeologist—a person who studies how people lived in ancient times.

archbishop—a Catholic or Anglican clergyman who supervises other bishops in a certain area.

artisan—a person who is skilled in a particular craft, such as a plumber, carpenter, silversmith, or mason.

assassination—the murder of a leader, who is suddenly or secretly attacked.

astronomy—the scientific study of stars, planets, and other heavenly bodies.

atheist—a person who does not believe in God.

awakening—a time when people are shaken up in their thinking and begin to look at life in a different way.

bachelor's degree—the award given by a college, university, or seminary to those who successfully complete its first level of study.

backwoods—a place some distance away from towns where nature is still wild and untamed.

bankrupt—a person who cannot pay his or her debts.

Baptist—a person who believes Christians should be dipped completely in water to show that they have died to their old life and risen to a new life in Christ.

baptize—to dip into or sprinkle with water as a sign that one's sins have been washed away.

baron—an English nobleman who had been given land directly by the king.

battlefront—a place where soldiers meet each other to fight.

belief—something that is thought to be true; an opinion.

benefactor—a person who helps another through acts of kindness or gifts of money.

Bill of Rights—the first ten amendments to the U.S. Constitution; laws that protect the basic rights of human beings.

bishop—the head of a district or diocese in the Roman Catholic or Anglican church.

bondage—being held under the control of another person; slavery.

bribe—money offered in exchange for someone doing something dishonest or against the law

bumpkin—a simple, crude person from the country.

Catholic—part of the church ruled by the Pope; Roman Catholic.

cause—a goal desired and worked toward by many people.

Cayuse (ki yus)—a member of a Native American tribe of Oregon and Washington.

chapel—a small building used for religious services.

chaplain—a member of the clergy who provides religious services for a military unit or an institution.

charitable—a person or group who provides help to the poor, sick, or needy.

charter—a written grant by a government to a person or group of people; a document that states the purpose of a group.

chief justice—the chairperson of a group of judges; the presiding judge of the U.S. Supreme Court.

Church of England—the name given to Episcopal Church in England; Anglican.

city councilman—a member of the advisory board of a town.

civil liberty—the freedom to enjoy the personal rights given to one by law without interference from the government.

coat of arms—a drawing of a shield which pictures the unique traits of a family, city, state, or country.

colonel—an officer who ranks above a lieutenant colonel and below a brigadier general.

colony—a group of people, such as the Pilgrims, who leave their own country to start a settlement in another land but continue as citizens of their homeland.

Committees of Correspondence—British colonists in America who wrote letters to keep the colonies up to date on how Great Britain was mistreating its colonies

Committee of Safety—British colonists in America who took responsibility for organizing local resistance to British military control of the colonies.

commonwealth—the people who make up a state.

communion—a group of people with the same religious beliefs; the religious ceremony known as Holy Communion, in which bread and wine are used to represent the body and blood of Jesus Christ.

compact—an agreement or contract.

compromise—a bargain between opponents where each gives up something they wanted in order to settle their argument.

Confederate States of America—a group of eleven southern states that set up their own government in 1860 and 1861.

Congregationalist—a member of a church which makes its own rules instead of being governed by bishops.

Congress—the elected lawmakers of the United States, including the Senate and House of Representatives.

conservative—a person who is extremely careful about making major changes.

constitution—a set of rules that control how a country, state or group is governed.

Continental—the American colonies who declared their independence from England; an American solider in the Revolutionary War.

converts—people who change from one belief to another; those who put their faith in Jesus Christ.

conviction—a strong belief about the rightness or wrongness of something.

covenant—a serious written agreement in which people promise to act toward each other in certain ways.

covered wagon—a means of transportation for American pioneers; a large wagon with a canvas top pulled by teams of horses, mules, or oxen.

crusade—an active and intense effort to change the way people believe and behave.

culture—the way people of a particular nationality, ethnic group or religion relate to each other.

daguerreotype—an early photograph engraved on a silver-coated copper plate.

debate—a discussion between people of different viewpoints or opinions in which a speaker for each side takes a turn.

debtor—one who fails to pay for something purchased or to repay borrowed money.

declaration—a public announcement.

Delaware—a member of a Native American tribe living in the Delaware valley; the language of this Algonquin tribe.

delegate—a representative chosen to speak and act for others.

democracy—a government in which decisions are made by the citizens.

Democrat—a member of one of the two main political parties in the United States.

denomination—a religious group, such as Baptists or Lutherans.

diplomat—a person who takes part in discussions and bargaining between nations.

Disciples of Christ—a religious group started in the U.S. in 1809 in an effort to return the Christian church to the model given in the New Testament.

dissenter—a person whose beliefs cause them to separate from the majority.

district attorney—a lawyer employed by the government to file suits against those who commit crimes.

divine right—the claim that kings get their power and authority directly from God and not from the people.

emancipation—the act or process of setting a person free from slavery.

engrave—to cut letters, numbers, and figures into metal.

enlist—to join the army.

epidemic—an illness that affects many people in a place at the same time.

equal rights—the fair and consistent treatment of all people in a society, regardless of their color, sex, religion, or beliefs.

etch—the use of acid to eat away lines on metal or glass, creating a picture or design.

evangelism—bringing people to personal faith in Jesus Christ.

expedition—a journey with a special purpose.

experiment—to test or try a theory or an invention.

exposition—a collection of public exhibits or shows.

federal—having to do with a strong central government.

feudal estates—areas of land belonging to lords during the Middle Ages; people served the lords in order to farm the land and to receive protection from enemy attacks.

founder—one who takes the first steps in building or starting something.

free trade—the freedom to buy merchandise from and sell merchandise to other countries without extreme government rules.

freedom of religion—the right to worship as one chooses without penalty or punishment.

frontier—the outer limit of settlement where there are no towns and the outdoor world is still wild.

furlough—permission for a soldier to leave the army for a short time.

general—a military officer ranking above a colonel.

Gospel—the teachings of Jesus Christ based on the first four books of the New Testament.

government—the way a nation rules itself and its citizens.

governor—a person elected or appointed as the head of a state or colony.

grammar school—in colonial America, a school where students learned Hebrew, Greek, and Latin along with proper English; later came to mean an elementary school.

grant—a gift of land or certain rights given by a king, queen, or government.

House of Burgesses—Colonial Virginia's assembly of elected representatives.

House of Representatives—the lower house of the U.S. Congress; a group of lawmakers.

Huguenots—French Protestants who were often persecuted during the 1500s and 1600s.

identification papers—official documents proving a person's standing as a free citizen of a particular country.

immigrant—a person who comes to make a home in a new country.

immoral—an action that goes against God's laws.

inauguration—the ceremony which officially begins a person's service in a public office.

indenture—a written agreement that requires someone to work for someone else in exchange for travel expenses or training in a particular occupation.

indivisible—unable to be divided or broken into separate parts.

injustice—without fairness.

innocent—not guilty of wrongdoing.

institute—a school designed to teach special subjects, such as art, science, or military training.

institution—any organization started for some public or social reason.

international—something that involves more than one country.

interpreter—a person who translates a foreign language so that those who don't speak it can understand and be understood.

invasion—the forced entry of a foreign army.

Iroquois (ir'uh kwoi)—a powerful Native American tribe that once lived mostly in New York.

Jehovah—an English word used in place of the unspeakable name (JHVH, or Yahweh) given to God by the Jews.

Jesuit—a priest in the Roman Catholic Society of Jesus, a group devoted to missionary and educational work.

justice—the practice of acting and making decisions in a fair way.

kingdom—a region ruled by a king or queen.

knight—a man especially honored for some service to his country; a title given by a king or queen.

land grant—a gift of land given by the government for a specific use.

lantern—a portable lamp with glass and metal sides and made to protect a flame from being blown out.

lava—liquid rock that flows from a volcano.

legislative assembly—a group of government leaders with the power to make laws.

liberate—to set free; release.

lieutenant—a military officer.

lieutenant colonel—a military officer above a lieutenant and below a colonel.

longboat—the largest boat carried by a sailing ship.

lord—a ruler, master, or chief.

lordship—a title used when speaking to or about a lord.

loyalty—faithfulness to a cause, a country, a person, or a belief.

Lutheran—a Protestant religious group started by Martin Luther.

magistrate—a government official who is responsible for upholding the law.

majority—a number more than half of the total.

massacre—the heartless killing of a group of people who are unable to or to defend themselves.

mast—a wooden pole attached to the deck of a ship to support the sails.

memorial—a monument or marker that reminds people of an important event or person.

Mennonite—a member of a Protestant group that practices a simple lifestyle and refuses acts of violence, including military service.

midway—the amusement section of a fair or carnival where games are played and food is sold.

militia—the physically able men in a town or area who can be called on to defend the place in an emergency.

minuteman—colonial Americans who promised to fight against the British as soon as they were called on.

mission—the home and central meeting place of a missionary group, often including a farm, school, and hospital.

missionary—a person sent by a religious group to teach others about the Bible and to improve their way of living.

mob—a group of excited people who can easily be stirred up to hurt someone or to destroy property.

Mohegan (mo 'he guhn)—a member of a Native American tribe originally living in Connecticut; Mohican.

monument—a statue or building that honors a person or group of people who did something worthy of special honor.

morals—the ways of thinking, speaking, and acting that a person believes are good, honest, and pure.

motto—a group of words that help to describe what something is about; an idea that guides and shapes an individual, family, or group of people.

Narrangansett (nar uh gan'sit)—a member of a Native American tribe that once lived primarily in Rhode Island.

National Archives—the government office responsible for preserving U.S. government records.

native land—the country a person was born in.

new birth—the new life given to those who receive Jesus Christ as the Son of God and the one who saves them from sin.

Nez Percé (nez 'purs)—a member of a Native American tribe whose homeland is located in Oregon, Washington, and Idaho.

oath of office—a solemn promise to faithfully do the job for which one has been chosen.

officer—a person in the army or other branch of the military who tells others what to do.

oppression—unfair or painful treatment; cruelty

orphanage—a large home for children without parents.

overthrow—to put an end to someone's power.

pamphlet—a small booklet with a paper cover; usually written about a subject of current interest.

parliament—a council or congress that makes laws.

parson—a minister.

pastor—a minister in charge of a church.

patent—a government document that protects the rights of an inventor; an invention that is guaranteed to be the first of its kind.

patriot—a person who loves and defends his or her country.

persecute—to treat badly or to hurt, especially because of someone's beliefs.

petition—asking someone in authority for permission to do something.

pew—a bench in a church.

philosophy—the study of the truth about human life and the universe.

pilgrim—a person who makes a journey because of their religious beliefs; a settler in Plymouth Colony.

pioneer—one of the first people to settle in a particular area.

pistol—a gun that is small enough to be held and fired with one hand.

plantation—a large farm on which cotton, tobacco, or sugar cane is grown.

pledge—a serious promise.

pneumonia—a disease of the lungs.

politician—a person who spends much of his or her time in the business of government, especially one who tries to win or keep a particular position in the government.

pope—the person of highest authority in the Roman Catholic Church.

powwow—a Native American ceremony with feasting, dancing, and religious rituals.

prairie—a large area of flat or slightly rolling grass land.

prejudice—an opinion toward someone or something that is not based on facts or careful research.

Presbyterian—a Protestant denomination that is controlled by elected leaders.

president—the head of a company, college, or country.

priest—a minister in a Roman Catholic, Anglican, or Episcopal church; a person who performs religious ceremonies.

principles—the basic truths, beliefs, and rules of a person or group.

prisoner of war—a person taken captive by the enemy during a war.

proclamation—an official public announcement.

profession—a kind of work that requires special education in a college or university.

professor—a teacher in a college or university.

proposal—a statement of how someone plans to do something.

prosperity—success; doing well.

Protestant—a member of any of the Christian churches that broke away from the Roman Catholic Church.

province—a main division of land in a country.

Puritans—a group in the Church of England who believed God wanted people to practice simple worship and to lead holy (pure) lives.

Quaker—member of a Christian group called the Society of Friends; one who sometimes began to shake or quake when feeling what was believed to be the presence of God.

quill—a large feather whose stiff tip was sharpened to a point and dipped in ink for writing.

rebel—a person who fights against authority.

recruit—a new soldier or sailor.

rector—a minister who has charge of a church district.

Redcoat—a British soldier in the Revolutionary War.

redemptioner—a person who buys back his or her freedom from service to a master.

reform—to make something better; to give something a new shape.

regiment—a large group of soldiers under the command of a colonel.

repent—to be sorry for doing wrong and to ask forgiveness.

representative—a person chosen to speak or act for others.

republic—a nation whose citizens choose representatives to manage the government.

Republican—a person who believes in government by elected leaders; a member of one of the two main political parties in the United States.

reputation—what people think about the honesty and goodness of a person.

resignation—a notice to quit given by a worker to his or her boss.

resolution—a formal statement of an opinion or belief.

reveler—one who enjoys having a good time; a rowdy party-goer.

Reverend—a title for a Christian minister.

revival—bringing something back to life or health.

revolution—an overthrow of a government.

rotunda—a round building or room with a dome.

Royal Governor—a head of a state chosen directly by a king or queen.

sacrifice—a gift made to God; to give up something of value.

saloon—a place where people go to buy and drink alcoholic beverages.

salvation—something or someone who sets another person free from sin and punishment.

Salvation Army—a group whose purpose is to spread Christianity and to help the needy.

Savior—Jesus Christ; one who saves others from punishment for their wrongdoing.

scholar—a student in a school; a person who has great knowledge about a certain subject.

schoolmaster—a man who teaches in a school; a principal.

Scriptures—the Bible.

seamstress—a skilled woman who makes money by sewing for others.

secession—to break away or pull out of a group.

Secretary of War—head of the government department responsible for military business.

segregate—to separate one racial group from another.

self-govern—to rule oneself.

seminary—a school where ministers are trained; a boarding school.

Senate—a group of high-ranking lawmakers.

session—a period of time in which a group meetings to do its regular business.

settler—a person who makes a home in a place where people have not lived before.

slavery—the practice of claiming other people as one's own property and demanding that they obey one's orders.

slum—the part of a town or city where poor people live in crowded, run-down buildings.

smallpox—a contagious disease that causes fever and red spots on the skin.

society—a community, nation, or large group of people who have common traditions, institutions, and similar interests or activities.

Sons of Liberty—a secret group of American patriots who gathered together in 1765 to resist what they believed were unfair British laws.

Spaniard—a person from Spain.

sponsor—a person or group that supports another person or group.

Stars and Stripes—a name for the flag of the United States.

state house—a building in which the lawmakers of a country or state meet to conduct their business.

statesman—a person who carries out the work of the government.

statue—a wood, metal, clay, or stone image of a famous person.

statute—a law.

steeple—the high tower on a church.

strategy—planning and managing something, especially a war.

sunbonnet—a hat worn by women to shade their faces from the sun.

Supreme Court—the highest court in the United States.

surgeon general—a military medical doctor.

surveyor—a person who measures an area of land and marks its location on a map.

tariff—taxes charged by a country on foreign-made products.

tavern—a place where people go to eat or drink.

taxation—the practice of collecting money from citizens to pay for government business and projects.

telegraph—a device used to send coded message through electrical wires.

temperance—the practice of consuming little or no alcoholic drinks.

territory—an area that is not yet a state but does have an organized government.

thanksgiving—words or actions that show people's gratitude for what they have received.

thatched—a roof made of straw, rushes, or palm leaves.

theology—a study of beliefs about God and religion.

tidewater—low-lying land along the coast of a sea.

tithe—one-tenth of a person's income; an amount of money given to the church.

tobacco—a plant whose leaves are used for smoking or chewing.

tomahawk—an ax used by Native Americans as a weapon and a tool.

tomb—a grave in which a dead body is placed.

town meeting—a meeting of votes in a town who gather to do public business.

U.S. Treasury—the part of the U.S. government which is responsible for collecting, spending, and guarding the nation's money.

treaty—an official agreement between two countries.

tribal elders—the older, more experienced leaders of a Native American tribe.

tutor—a private teacher.

typhoid fever—a disease caused by unclean water or food.

tyranny—the cruel or unfair use of power by those in control.

uppity—arrogant, stuck up, self-centered.

valor—courage.

values—the qualities considered most important in a person's life.

vice president—the person next in importance to the president, and who takes over if the president dies or becomes too sick to do his job.

vigilance—the condition of staying alert and watchful for any signs of trouble or wrongdoing.

Vikings—ancient Scandinavian sailors who explored, attacked, and raided the coasts of Europe.

virtue—personal qualities such as kindness, honesty, honor, goodness.

Wampanoag (wam puh no'ag)—member of a Native American tribe that lived in Massachusetts.

waterways—rivers, streams, and lakes where boats can travel.

wigwam—a Native American house made of arched wooden poles, animal skins, and tree bark.

wilderness—a place where no one lives.

worship—to show great honor and respect toward someone, especially God.

Yankee—a person born or living in the northern part of the United States during the Civil War; an American colonist at the time of the War for Independence from Great Britain.

YMCA—Young Men's Christian Association; a group started by business leaders and ministers who wanted to give young men a place to meet in the cities that offered a more healthy atmosphere than the saloons.

BIBLIOGRAPHY

Adler, Mortimer J., ed. *The Annals of America.* 18 vols. Chicago: Encyclopedia Britannica, 1976.

Ahlstrom, Sydney E. *A Religious History of the American People.* 2 vols. Garden City, NY: Image Books, 1975.

Akers, Charles W. *Abigail Adams, An American Woman.* Boston: Little, Brown & Co., 1980.

Andrist, Ralph K., ed. *George Washington: A Biography in His Own Words.* New York: Newsweek, 1972.

Bakeless, Katherine and John. *Signers of the Declaration.* Boston: Houghton Mifflin, 1969.

Baning, Lance. *The Sacred Fire of Liberty: James Madison and the Founding of the Federal Republic.* New York: Cornell University, 1995.

Bernard, Jacqueline. *Journey toward Freedom.* New York: Thistle, Grosset & Dunlap, 1967.

The Bible in Schools. Garland, TX: American Tract Society, 1995.

Biel, Timothy Levi. *The Civil War.* San Diego: Lucent Books, 1991.

Brentano, Frances. *Nations Under God.* New York: Channel Press, 1957.

Brown, Fern G. *James A. Garfield, 20th President of the United States.* Ada, OK: Garrett Educational Corp, 1990.

"Charles Grandison Finney, 19th Century Giant of Revivalism." *Christian History* Volume VII, #4, Issue 20.

Chidsey, Donald Barr. *Sam Adams.* New York: Crown, 1965.

Coulter, Tony. *La Salle and the Explorers of the Mississippi.* New York: Chelsea, 1991.

Cousins, Norman. *In God We Trust.* New York: Harper & Bros., 1958.

Dayton, Donald W. *Discovering an Evangelical Heritage.* New York: Harper and Row, 1976.

Dolan, Sean. *Junípero Serra.* New York: Chelsea House, 1991.

Donal, David Herbert. *Lincoln.* New York: Simon & Schuster, 1995.

Douglas, J. D. with Philip W. Comfort and Donald Mitchell. *Who's Who in Christian History.* Wheaton, IL: Tyndale, 1992.

Douglass, Frederick. *Autobiographies.* New York: The Library of America, 1994.

Dowley, Tim, ed. *The History of Christianity.* Batavia, IL: Lion, 1977.

DuBois, William E. B. *Black Reconstruction.* New York: Russell & Russell, 1963.

Epler, Percy H. *The Life of Clara Barton.* New York: Macmillan, 1917.

Farquhar, Michael. "Old Maryland Is Born Again at Historic St. Mary's City," *The Washington Post* (October 11,1995).

Federer, William J. *America's God and Country Encyclopedia of Quotations.* Coppel, TX: FAME Publishing, Inc., 1994.

Ferris, Robert G. *Founders and Frontiersmen: Historic Places Commemorating Early Nationhood and the Westward Movement, 1783-1828.* Washington: U.S. Department of the Interior, National Park Service, 1967.

Ferris, Robert G. *Signers of the Constitution.* U.S. Department of the Interior, National Park Service, 1976.

Ferris, Robert G. *Signers of the Declaration.* Washington: U.S. Department of the Interior, National Park Service, 1973.

Fischer, David Hackett. *Paul Revere's Ride*. New York: Oxford University, 1994.

Fishwick, Marshall W. *Illustrious Americans: Clara Barton*. Silver Burdett, 1966.

Gaustad, Edwin S. *A Documentary History of Religion in America*. 2 vols. Grand Rapids, MI: William B. Eerdmans Publishing Co., 1982.

Greenfield, Eloise. *Mary McLeod Bethune*. New York: Thomas Y. Crowell, 1977.

Goodyear, Lucille J. "The Pledge of Allegiance," *Highlights for Children*, June 1988.

Gordon, Anna. *The Beautiful Life of Frances Willard*. Chicago: Women's Temperance Union Publishing Assoc., 1898.

Hammack, Mary L. *A Dictionary of Women in Church History*. Chicago: Moody, 1984.

Hubner, Mary. "The Clara Barton Legend," *History News*, May, 1981.

James, Edward T. *Notable American Women, 1607-1950: A Biographical Dictionary*. Cambridge: Belknap, Harvard University Press, 1971).

Kelso, Richard. *Building a Dream: Mary Bethune's School*. Austin, TX: Stech-Vaughn, 1993.

Lerner, Gerda. *The Woman in American History*. Menlo Park, CA: Addison-Wesley, 1971.

Lillegard, Dee. *James A. Garfield*. Chicago: Childrens Press, 1987.

Loomis, Albertine. *Grapes of Canaan, Hawaii 1820*. Honolulu: Hawaiian Children's Mission Society, 1951).

Lotz, Philip Henry. *Women Leaders*. New York: Association Press, 1940.

Marrin, Albert. *Virginia's General: Robert E. Lee and the Civil War*. New York: Atheneum, 1994.

Marshall, Peter, and David Manuel. *The Light and the Glory*. Old Tappan, NJ: Flemming H. Revell, 1986.

Marshall, Peter, and David Manuel. *Sea to Shining Sea*. Old Tappan, NJ: Flemming H. Revell, 1977.

Mason, F. Van Wyck. *The Maryland Colony*. New York: Macmillan, 1969.

Meade, Robert Douthat. *Patrick Henry: Patriot in the Making*. Philadelphia: J.B. Lippincott, 1957.

Meade, Robert Douthat. *Patrick Henry: Practical Revolutionary*. Philadelphia: J.B. Lippincott, 1969.

Meadows, Denis. *Five Remarkable Englishmen*. New York: Devin-Adair, 1961.

Meltzer, Milton. *Mary McLeod Bethune, Voice of Black Hope*. New York: Viking Kestrel, 1987.

Morris, Richard B. *Seven Who Shaped Our Destiny*. New York: Harper and Row, 1973.

Morris, Richard B. *Witnesses at the Creation. Hamilton, Madison, Jay and the Constitution*. New York: Holt, Rinehard & Winston, 1985.

Myers, Elisabeth P. *Katherine Lee Bates, Girl Poet*. Indianapolis: Bobbs-Merrill, 1961.

Reid, Daniel G., et al, eds. *Dictionary of Christianity in America*. Downers Grove, IL: Intervarsity Press, 1990.

Russell, Sharman Apt. *Frederick Douglass, Abolitionist Editor*. New York: Chelsea, 1988.

Sarles, Frank B. Jr. and Charles E. Shedd. *Colonials and Patriots: Historic Places Commemorating Our Forebears, 1700-1783*. Washington: U.S. Department of the Interior, National Park Service, 1964.

Scott, John Anthony. *Settlers on the Eastern Shore*. New York: Alfred Knopf, 1967.

"Spiritual Awakenings in North America," *Christian History* (Volume 8, No. 3, Issue 23).

Stout, Harry S. *The Divine Dramatist: George Whitefield and the Rise of Modern Evangelicalism*. Grand Rapids, MI: Eerdmans, 1992.

Tebbel, John William. *George Washington's America*. New York: E.P. Dutton, 1954.

Tilton, Rafael. *The Importance of Clara Barton*. San Diego: Lucent Books, 1995.

Trueblood, Elton. *Abraham Lincoln: Theologian of American Anguish*. New York: Harper, 1973.

Tucker, Ruth. *From Jerusalem to Irian Jaya*. Grand Rapids, MI: Academie, Zondervan, 1983.

Wheelock, Eleazar. *Memoirs of the Rev. Eleazar Wheelock, D.D.* Newburyport: Little & Co., 1811.

Willard, Frances E. *Glimpses of Fifty Years*. New York: National Temperance Society, 1889.

Wolfe, Rinna Evelyn. *Mary McLeod Bethune*. New York: Franklin Watts, 1992.

Woodbridge, John D., ed. *Great Leaders of the Christian Church*. Chicago: Moody, 1988.